ACADEMIC ENCOUNTERS

CONTENT
FOCUS

Human Behavior

ACADEMIC ENCOUNTERS

Reading, Study Skills, and Writing

CONTENT
FOCUS

Human Behavior

BERNARD SEAL

CAMBRIDGE
UNIVERSITY PRESS

Published by the Press Syndicate of the University of Cambridge
The Pitt Building, Trumpington Street, Cambridge CB2 1RP, United Kingdom

Cambridge University Press
40 West 20th Street, New York, NY 10011-4211, USA
10 Stamford Road, Oakleigh, Melbourne 3166, Australia

First published 1997

Printed in the United States of America

Library of Congress Cataloging-in-Publication Data

Seal, Bernard.
Academic encounters : reading, study skills, and writing : content focus, human behavior /
Bernard Seal.
p. cm.
ISBN 0-521-47658-5
1. English language—Textbooks for foreign speakers. 2. Human behavior —Problems, exercises, etc. 3. English language—Rhetoric.
4. Readers—Human behavior. 5. Academic writing. 6. College readers. I. Title.
PE1128.S37 1997   97-3664
428.2′4—dc20   CIP

A catalog record for this book is available from the British Library

ISBN 0-521-47658-5 paperback

Book design and text composition by Jill Little, *Mediamark*
Line drawings by *Suffolk Technical Illustrators, Inc.*

To the memory of my parents
Eli and Ethel

Contents

UNIT ONE Mind, Body, and Health 1

Chapter 1: The Influence of Mind Over Body

Chapter 2: Preventing Illness

Chapter 8: The Language of Touch, Space, and Artifacts

UNIT FIVE *Interpersonal Relationships* 177

Chapter 9: Friendship

Author's
Acknowledgments

Acknowledgments for a book such as this are due to people in three distinct areas: the publishing house, the school, and the home.

First, publishers. Going way back, I must acknowledge the role played by Susan Ryan. She saw an early sample of the manuscript and believed in it from the start. Thanks are then due to Laurie Likoff, for taking the project as far as she could. Mary Vaughn, at Cambridge University Press, I thank for all her hard work, guidance, and solid support. Also at Cambridge I acknowledge the invaluable assistance of Mary Carson and Sue André. Thanks, too, to the Cambridge reviewers. Jane Mairs, however, must receive the most credit. Her penetrating eye and blue pencil have helped shape much of the look and content of this book.

And so to school. Thanks to those who piloted earlier versions of the book and provided valuable feedback on their experiences: Gay Brookes at Borough of Manhattan Community College; Laura LeDréan at the University of Houston, ELI; Elaine McVey at San Diego State University, ALI; Barry O'Sullivan at Okayama Daigaku, School of Education, Japan; Deborah Phillips at LCP International Institute, Redlands; and Deanna Wormuth at Texas A&M University.

Special thanks also to all my colleagues at the American Language Institute at the University of Southern California. Early versions of the book were extensively piloted by many teachers, but I particularly want to acknowledge the help of Daryl Kinney, Alain Martinossi, and Karen Schmitt, who discussed the book at length with me and provided me with copious notes. I also want to thank my colleagues David Bycina, Mary Alvin, Cheryl Kraft, and the late Frank Diffley - all of whom were instrumental in shaping my ideas on content-based instruction. And, of course, one must not forget administrators. Dave Eskey and Lisa Patriquin demonstrated their support by setting me up with helpful teaching schedules and by providing me with leaves of absence when needed.

And finally, thanks are due to my family. My children, Daniel and Elliott, provide a delightful distraction from my work and are ever an inspiration to me. And my wife, Chris, has played a dual role. She is both an exemplary colleague at work and a wonderful, supportive partner at home.

Introduction

To the Instructor

The approach

Academic Encounters adopts a content-based approach to academic English instruction. Students are presented with authentic samples of text taken from North American college textbooks. They then study these texts to develop their reading and study skills. The high interest content of the texts also provides prompts for student writing assignments.

The source material

There are five units in *Academic Encounters* and each is based on material taken from either a psychology or human communications textbook that has been used in regular university or community college courses in North America. The textbook material has been abridged and occasionally reorganized, but on the sentence level little of the language has been changed. Each unit of *Academic Encounters* is divided into two chapters, with four readings in each chapter. Each reading is one to four pages long.

The level

Although *Academic Encounters* is based on authentic college-level material, it is not intended for the most advanced ESL student. The student who will benefit most from this course will be at the intermediate to high intermediate level. This student may well be encountering academic text in English for the first time. However, the readings are short enough and the tasks sufficiently well scaffolded to allow a student at this level to access the texts successfully.

The content

The content of each unit of *Academic Encounters* focuses on some aspect of human behavior. The fact that the book has a unified thematic content throughout has several advantages. First, it gives the students a realistic sense of studying a course at a university, in which each week's assignments are related to and build on each other. Second, as language and concepts recur, the students begin to feel that the readings are getting easier, building their confidence as readers of academic text. Finally, after studying the book, some students may feel that they have enough background in the subject matter to actually take a course in psychology or human communications to fulfill part of their general education requirements.

The skills

The main goal of *Academic Encounters* is to give students the skills and the confidence to approach a piece of academic text, read it efficiently and critically, and extract the main ideas and key details. But the goal of academic reading is not just to retrieve information. It is often even more important for a student to be able to display that knowledge in a test-taking situation. For this reason, students are taught highlighting, note-taking and test-taking preparation skills. An additional goal of *Academic Encounters* is the development of students' academic writing. Writing skills as well as reading and study skills are developed in tasks that accompany each reading and that appear in two separate sections: "Preparing to Read" and "After you Read."

Preparing to Read tasks

Each reading in *Academic Encounters* has one page of prereading tasks. Prereading is heavily emphasized since it is regarded as a crucial step in the reading process. Some of the prereading activities teach students how to quickly get a good overall idea of the content. Students also learn to skim for main ideas and to survey the text for headings, graphic material and terms in boldface, all of which can provide important content clues. Another type of prereading task has students think about the topic of the reading, predict its content, and recall their prior knowledge and personal experiences to help them assimilate the new information they are about to encounter in the reading.

After You Read tasks

After reading a text there are different types of tasks that students may be asked to perform. Some of these ask students to demonstrate their understanding of the text, either by answering reading comprehension questions or by performing a task such as drawing a graph or performing a role play. Other tasks ask students to reflect on the content and deepen their understanding of the text by personalizing the information. Some tasks ask students to analyze the structure of the text, looking for main ideas, supporting details, and authorial commentary. There are language tasks which focus on vocabulary and others which focus on some of the salient grammatical features of the text. Students learn how to highlight a text, take notes in the margins and in a notebook, and practice test-taking skills. The rich variety of tasks and task types allows students to experiment with different study skill strategies and to discover their learning style preferences.

Writing

There are plentiful and varied opportunities in *Academic Encounters* for students to practice their writing skills. These vary from prompts for essay writing, text summaries, and journal writing to writing short answers to test questions. At the same time, as students continually read and analyze academic English, they will begin to acquire insight into its organization and style, and their own writing will begin to develop a more academic tone.

Student interaction

Many of the tasks in the book are divided into steps. Some of these steps are to be done by the student working alone, others by the students in pairs or in small groups, still others by the teacher with the whole class. To make the book as lively as possible, student interaction has been built into most activities. Thus, although *Academic Encounters* is a reading, study skills, and writing book, speaking activities abound. Students discuss the content of the texts before and after reading them; they often work collaboratively to solve task problems; they perform role play activities and they frequently compare answers in pairs or small groups.

Task commentary boxes

When a task type occurs for the first time in the book, it is headed by a colored commentary box that explains what skill is being practiced and why it is important. When the task occurs again later in the book, it may be accompanied by another commentary box, either as a reminder or to present new information about the skill. At the back of the book, there is an alphabetized index of all the tasks. Page references in boldface indicate tasks that are headed by commentary boxes.

Design features

A great deal of attention has been paid to design features in this book. There are two types of pages: text pages and task pages. Task pages are clearly differentiated from text pages by a colored vertical bar that runs along the outside edge of the page. The task pages contain the activities that students are asked to do either before or after reading the text. Tasks and texts never occur on the same page, and the text pages have been designed to look as much as possible like authentic university textbook pages. This helps to create a sense for students that they are actually reading from a university textbook. The readings and tasks have been carefully laid out so that each new reading begins on a right-hand page, opposite one page of prereading tasks. These design features make the book easy to use.

Order of units

The units do not have to be taught in the order in which they appear in the book, although this order is recommended. To a certain extent, tasks do build upon each other so that, for example, a note-taking task later in the book may draw upon information that has been offered in an earlier unit. Teachers who want to teach the units out of order, however, may do so. They can use the task index at the back of the book to see what information has been presented in earlier units and build that information into their lessons. In terms of reading topics, also, the order of the units is regarded as optimal, especially for students who have recently arrived in North America. Many of these students are under great stress and thus find the first unit particularly useful since it deals with how to manage stress and stay healthy. The final unit, too, can be done only when students feel comfortable with each other, since it deals with more intimate topics such as friendship and love.

Course length

Each of the five units of *Academic Encounters* contains a unit preview section and eight readings, and represents approximately 16-20 hours of classroom material. *Academic Encounters* could thus be a suitable course book for a 64- to 80-hour course (when a teacher selects four of the five units) or an 80- to 100-hour course (when all the units are used). The course can, however, be made shorter or longer. To shorten the course, teachers might choose not to do every task in the book and to assign some tasks and texts as homework, rather than do them in class. To lengthen the course, teachers might choose to supplement the book with some content-related material from their own files and to spend more time developing students' writing skills.

TO THE STUDENT

Welcome to *Academic Encounters*! In this book, all the text material that you will encounter has been taken from textbooks used in regular North American university or community college courses. *Academic Encounters* will teach you how to become a more efficient and competent reader of such texts and provide you with the study skills that you will need to be successful in an American university classroom.

Texts that appear in college textbooks are different from other types of texts that you may have read in English. They are organized differently and are written in a distinctive style. Since a great deal of effort has gone into making the texts in *Academic Encounters* look and read exactly as they might in an academic textbook, by studying this book you will have an excellent opportunity to become familiar with the special features and style of academic text.

The approach in *Academic Encounters* may be different from what you are used to. First, you are asked to try to master the subject matter, as if you were studying in a regular university course. Then, after having studied the texts and having read them critically, you are taught the skills that would allow you to retrieve the information you have learned in a test-taking situation. For example, you are taught highlighting, note-taking, and test preparation skills.

Although the primary emphasis in the book is on reading and study skills, there are also opportunities to study the language of the texts. It is particularly important as you get ready to study in an English-speaking university that you broaden your vocabulary, and many of the activities are designed to help you do so. Sometimes, too, the focus of instruction is on a grammatical structure that commonly occurs in academic text.

There are also plentiful opportunities in *Academic Encounters* for you to practice your academic writing skills. You will find that by continually reading and studying academic English your own academic writing will improve. As you become more and more familiar with academic texts, how they are organized, and the language in which they are written, you will find yourself naturally beginning to adopt a more academic writing style of your own.

The texts in this book all come from the academic disciplines of psychology and human communications. One effect of studying subject matter that comes only from these fields is that you will build up a lot of new knowledge in these areas. Some international undergraduates, after using this book, feel that they have had enough background information in the subject matter to go on and take an introductory course in psychology or human communications to fulfill part of their general education requirements. Perhaps you, too, will gain the knowledge and confidence to do the same at some future date.

Finally, we hope that you find this book to be not only useful, but enjoyable. The topics have all been chosen for their high interest, and you have been given plentiful opportunities to discuss them with your classmates. It is important to remember in all your studies that the most successful learning takes place when you enjoy what you are studying and find it interesting.

UNIT 1

Mind, Body, and Health

In this unit we look at the relationship between human behavior and health. In Chapter 1, we examine research that shows that our mental and emotional states, especially feelings of stress, may influence our physical health. In Chapter 2, we see that illness can sometimes be prevented or controlled by changing people's behavior, for example by helping people relax, avoid smoking, or stay on an exercise program.

PREVIEWING THE UNIT

> **B**efore reading a unit (or chapter) of a textbook, it is a good idea to preview the contents page and think about the topics that will be covered. This will give you an overview of how the whole unit is organized and what it is going to be about.

Read the contents page for Unit 1 and answer the following questions.

Chapter 1: The influence of mind over body

1➤ The focus of the first three sections in Chapter 1 is the topic of stress. Work with a partner and make lists for the three following categories. Be prepared to explain your choices to the class.

- Five stressful jobs
- Five unstressful jobs
- Five illnesses frequently caused by stress

2➤ In Section 4 of this chapter you will read about how psychological states can affect the progress of the disease of cancer. Work with a partner and decide if the following statements are true (T) or false (F).

___ *1* Cancer is the leading cause of death in the United States.
___ *2* Many studies have shown that a stressful life-style is likely to cause cancer in humans.
___ *3* Once people get cancer, there is evidence to suggest that one's emotional state can change the development of the disease.

Chapter 2: Preventing illness

1➤ In the first three sections of Chapter 2, heart disease, smoking, and exercise are shown to be related topics. If smokers could quit smoking and more people took up regular exercise, there would be a great deal less heart disease.

   Work with a partner and interview each other for a few minutes on the topics of smoking and exercise. Ask questions such as:

1 Is smoking common in your country? Do you smoke? If yes, how many cigarettes per day? When did you start? If not, have you ever smoked and managed to quit? How did you quit?

2 What forms of exercise are popular in your country? Do you exercise much? What do you do?

2➤ Section 4 in Chapter 2 presents a definition of wellness. Change partners and interview each other about what you each do to keep fit and healthy.

UNIT CONTENTS

PREPARING TO READ

Thinking about the topic

> Thinking about a topic before you read helps provide a context for the reading and can make it easier to understand.

According to a famous study conducted by psychologists Holmes and Rahe, different life events can be rated according to the amount of stress they are likely to cause. Holmes and Rahe worked out a system in which the most stressful event (the death of a husband or wife) was given a value of 100 points; less stressful events were given values ranging from 99 to 1 points.

1➤ Look at the events listed. In the left-hand column, rank the events from most stressful (1) to least stressful (8). Compare answers with a classmate and explain why you rated one event to be more stressful than another.

Rank		Value
_____	getting married	_____
_____	changing to a new school	_____
_____	the death of a family member	_____
_____	going on vacation	_____
_____	being fired from work	_____
_____	getting divorced	_____
_____	getting a parking ticket	_____
_____	gaining a new family member	_____

2➤ Now, with your partner, agree on a value for each stressful event, using the Holmes and Rahe 100-point scale. Write this value in the column on the right.

3➤ Turn to Figure A, on page 9, where you will see the values that Holmes and Rahe gave to different events. Compare your values with theirs and discuss what surprises you in their list.

4➤ Discuss to what extent you think that if the same research were done in your country, instead of the United States, the results would be different.

NOW READ

Now read the text "What Is Stress?" When you finish, turn to the tasks that begin on page 7.

CHAPTER 1

The Influence of Mind Over Body

1 WHAT IS STRESS?

The term **stress** has been defined in several different ways. Sometimes the term is applied to stimuli or events in our environment that make physical and emotional demands on us, and sometimes it is applied to our emotional and physical reactions to such stimuli. In this discussion, we will refer to the environmental stimuli or events as **stressors** and to emotional and physical reactions as stress.

Many sorts of events can be stressors, including disasters such as hurricanes or tornadoes, major life events such as divorce or the loss of a job, and daily hassles such as having to wait in line at the supermarket when you need to be somewhere else in ten minutes. What all these events have in common is that they interfere with or threaten our accustomed way of life. When we encounter such stressors, we must pull together our mental and physical resources in order to deal with the challenge. How well we succeed in doing so will determine how serious a toll the stress will take on our mental and physical well-being.

REACTING TO STRESSORS

The Canadian physiologist Hans Seyle has been the most influential researcher and writer on stress. Seyle has proposed that both humans and other animals react to any stressor in three stages, collectively known as the *general adaptation syndrome*. The first stage, when the person or animal first becomes aware of the stressor, is the *alarm reaction*. In this stage, the organism becomes highly alert and aroused, energized by

stress
an emotional or physical reaction to demanding events or stimuli

stressor
an event or stimulus that causes stress

Any event – negative or positive – that causes a significant change in your everyday life may be stressful.

a burst of epinephrine. After the alarm reaction comes the stage of *resistance*, as the organism tries to adapt to the stressful stimulus or to escape from it. If these efforts are successful, the state of the organism returns to normal. If the organism cannot adapt to continuing stress, however, it enters a stage of *exhaustion* or collapse.

Seyle developed his model of the general adaptation syndrome as a result of research with rats and other animals. In rats, certain stressors, such as painful tail-pulling, consistently lead to the same sorts of stress reactions. In humans, however, it is harder to predict what will be stressful to a particular person at a particular time. Whether a particular stimulus will be stressful depends on the person's subjective appraisal of that stimulus. How threatening is it? How well have I handled this sort of thing in the past? How well will I be able to handle it this time? For one person, being called upon to give a talk in front of a class is a highly stressful stimulus that will immediately produce such elements of an alarm reaction as a pounding heart and a dry mouth. For another person, being called on to give a talk is not threatening at all, but facing a deadline to complete a term paper is extremely stressful. In humans, moreover, the specific stress reaction is likely to vary widely; some stressful situations give rise predominantly to emotions of fear, some to anger, some to helplessness and depression.

AFTER YOU READ

Task 1   Highlighting

> **H**ighlighting makes important information stand out so that you can find it easily when you go back to the text to study for a test. Systematically using different-colored highlighter pens can make the review process even easier. For example, you can use one color for key terms, another for definitions, another for names and dates, and so on.

1▶ Find the following words and phrases and highlight them.
- stress
- stressor
- the general adaptation syndrome
- alarm reaction
- resistance
- exhaustion

2▶ Use a different-colored highlighter and highlight the following:
- a definition of stress and stressors
- a statement about what all stressors have in common
- a description of stage 1 of the general adaptation syndrome
- a description of stage 2 of the general adaptation syndrome
- the sentence containing the main idea of the last paragraph

3▶ Compare your answers with a classmate's answers to see whether you have highlighted the same portions of text.

Task 2   Building vocabulary: Guessing meaning from context

> **A**lthough there may be many words in a text that you do not know, you do not want to continually stop and look up words in the dictionary. It is often possible to get a general idea of the meaning of a word or phrase (and that is all you really need in order to continue reading) by looking at its full context. This means that your eyes may have to travel back to the sentences that come before the word/phrase or forward to the sentence or sentences that follow it.

Read the following passages from the text and use the context to work out what the words in bold probably mean.

> Many sorts of events can be stressors, including disasters such as **hurricanes or tornadoes**, major life events such as divorce or the loss of a job, and **daily hassles** such as having to wait in line at the supermarket when you need to be somewhere else in ten minutes. What all these events **have in common** is that they interfere with or threaten our accustomed way of life.

hurricanes or tornadoes _____

daily hassles _____

to have something in common _____

Seyle has proposed that both human and other animals react to any stressor in three stages, **collectively** known as the *general adaptation syndrome*. The first stage, when the person or animal first becomes aware of the stressor, is the *alarm reaction*. In this stage, the organism becomes highly **alert and aroused**, energized by **a burst of epinephrine**.

collectively _____

alert and aroused _____

a burst of epinephrine _____

Whether a particular stimulus will be stressful depends on the person's **subjective appraisal** of that stimulus. How **threatening** is it? How well have I **handled** this sort of thing in the past? How well will I be able to handle it this time? For one person, **being called upon** to give a talk in front of a class is a highly stressful stimulus that will immediately produce such elements of an alarm reaction as a pounding heart and a dry mouth.

subjective appraisal _____

threatening _____

to handle _____

to be called upon _____

Task 3 Test-taking: Preparing for a short-answer quiz

One of the best ways to prepare for a short-answer quiz is to write down questions you think the professor will ask. Remember that your professor will probably ask different types of questions, not just questions that ask you to recall information (Type 1 questions).

Some short-answer question types

Type 1: Questions about data
These are what, when, how, where, and who questions. They ask you to define, list, locate, identify, recall, describe, and so on.

Type 2: Questions that develop concepts from the data
These questions ask you to discuss the data, point to relationships between different parts of the data, compare and contrast, analyze, predict, and so on.

Type 3: Questions that call for critical judgment
These questions ask you to evaluate, rank, rate, or assess aspects of the data, and to justify your answer.

1➤ Write four questions that you think a professor might ask about this text on a short-answer quiz. Try to use all three question types.

2► Exchange questions with a partner. Answer each other's questions orally and then discuss with your partner whether the answers were satisfactory or not.

Task 4 Test-taking: Writing short answers to test questions

> **I**n addition to practicing guessing which questions will be on a test, it is useful to practice writing the answers to them under time pressure.

1► With your partner, choose the two best questions that you and your partner thought of in Task 3. Give yourselves a reasonable time limit and write answers to the questions.

2► Read each other's answers and decide how complete the answers are.

Refer to "Thinking About the Topic" on page 4 for discussion relating to the figure below.

Life Event	Mean Value
Death of a spouse	100
Divorce	73
Death of a close family member	63
Major personal injury or illness	53
Marriage	50
Being fired from work	47
Retiring from work	45
Major change in health of a family member	44
Pregnancy	40
Gaining a new family member (*e.g., through birth, adoption, etc.*)	39
Major change in financial state (*e.g., having a lot more or less money*)	38
Death of a close friend	37
Taking out a mortgage or loan for a major purchase (*e.g., a home or business*)	31
Major change in responsibilities at work (*e.g., promotion, demotion*)	29
Son or daughter leaving home (*e.g., marriage, attending college*)	29
Beginning or ceasing formal schooling	26
Major changes in living conditions (*e.g., building a home, remodeling a home*)	25
Trouble with the boss	23
Major change in working hours or conditions	20
Change in residence	20
Changing to a new school	20
Taking out a small loan (*e.g., for a car, TV, freezer, etc.*)	17
Vacation	13
Christmas	12
Minor violations of the law (*e.g., traffic tickets, jaywalking*)	11

Figure A The Holmes and Rahe social readjustment rating scale (adapted from Holmes and Rahe, 1970)

PREPARING TO READ

Building vocabulary: Synonyms and antonyms

Learning a large number of words relating to a specific topic makes reading on that topic much easier. Knowing synonyms and antonyms is one way to build a topic-based vocabulary.

The following health-related words occur in this text. Find five pairs of near synonyms and two pairs of near antonyms.

a disease	be depressed	an illness
to be anxious	stress	to feel well
pressure	to suffer from	harmful
a pain	to be sick	to be afflicted with
an ache	helpful	

Synonyms

1 _____ is similar in meaning to _____
2 _____ is similar in meaning to _____
3 _____ is similar in meaning to _____
4 _____ is similar in meaning to _____
5 _____ is similar in meaning to _____

Antonyms

6 _____ is nearly opposite in meaning to _____
7 _____ is nearly opposite in meaning to _____

Scanning

Scanning involves looking quickly through a text to find a specific word or piece of information. There are often times when it's necessary to do this, such as when studying for a test or writing a paper, so it's a useful skill to practice.

This text deals with the relationship between being under stress and becoming ill. Scan the text quickly to find the following:

- illnesses that may be caused by stress (1st paragraph)
- jobs that are highly stressful (2nd paragraph)
- things people do when they are under stress that are not good for their health (3rd paragraph)

NOW READ

Now read the text "Stress and Illness." When you finish, turn to the tasks that begin on page 12.

2 STRESS AND ILLNESS

In many stressful situations, the body's responses can improve our performance – we become more energetic, more alert, better able to take effective action. But when stress is encountered continually, the body's reactions are more likely to be harmful than helpful to us. As will be seen later in this unit, the continual speeding up of bodily reactions and the production of stress-related hormones seem to make people more susceptible to heart disease. And stress reactions can reduce the disease-fighting effectiveness of the body's immune system, thereby increasing susceptibility to illnesses ranging from colds to cancer. Other diseases that can result at least in part from stress include arthritis, asthma, migraine headaches, and ulcers. Workers who experience the greatest degree of job pressures have been found to be especially likely to suffer from a large number of illnesses (House, 1981). Moreover, many studies have shown that people who have experienced major changes in their lives are at unusually high risk for a variety of illnesses.

People who have very stressful jobs may be more susceptible to illness.

As an example of stress-induced illness, take the case of stomach ulcers, small lesions in the stomach wall that afflict one out of twenty people at some point in their lives. Ulcers are a common disorder among people who work in occupations that make heavy psychological demands, from assembly-line workers to air-traffic controllers. In many cases, stress is the culprit. Stress leads to increased secretion of hydrochloric acid in the stomach. Hydrochloric acid normally helps to break down foods during digestion, but in excess amounts it can eat away at the stomach lining, producing ulcers.

Stress may also contribute to disease in less direct ways, by influencing moods and behavior. People under stress may become anxious or depressed and as a result may eat too much or too little, have sleep difficulties, smoke or drink more, or fail to exercise. These behavioral changes may, in turn, be harmful to their health. In addition, people are more likely to pay attention to certain bodily sensations, such as aches and pains, when they are under stress and to decide that they are "sick." If the person were not under stress, the same bodily sensations might not be perceived as symptoms and the person might continue to feel "well." Some researchers have suggested that assuming the role of a "sick person" is one way in which certain people try to cope with stress (Cohen, 1979). Instead of dealing with the stressful situation directly, these people fall sick. After all, it is often more acceptable in our society to be sick and to seek medical help than it is to admit that one cannot cope with the stresses of life.

AFTER YOU READ

Task 1 Language focus: Paraphrasing causality

In your writing you may include someone else's ideas, but not their exact words (unless you cite the source and use quotation marks). It is important, therefore, to learn to paraphrase. Many students think that the way to paraphrase is simply to use synonyms. In fact this is only one of the steps involved in writing a paraphrase. You must first understand the sense relations in a sentence. Then you can restructure the sentence and express the sense relations in another way.

The sense relations in many of the sentences in this text involve causality, or cause and effect. Causality may be expressed in many different ways in English, as you can see from the examples in the following table.

Cause	Effect
X causes	Y
X leads to	Y
When X happens,	Y happens.
X happens,	thereby causing Y.
X happens,	thus causing Y.
X happens.	This results in Y.
X happens.	As a result, Y happens.
X happens.	Consequently, Y happens.
X happens.	For this reason, Y happens.

Note that more tentative language is often used when expressing the effect of X, for example: X may lead to Y; When X happens, Y is likely to happen.

1➤ In note form, causality is often indicated with an arrow. Turn the following notes into full sentences using some of the different ways of expressing causality listed in the table. A sample answer has been provided for the first example.

1 too much stress ⟶ breakdown of the immune system ⟶ susceptible to disease

Too much stress may lead to a breakdown in the immune system. As a result, people may become more susceptible to disease.

2 stress ⟶ too much secretion of hydrochloric acid ⟶ ulcers

3 stress ⟶ mood changes ⟶ depression ⟶ too much smoking and drinking ⟶ illnesses

4 stress ⟶ attention to bodily reactions ⟶ people may decide they are sick

2➤ The following sentences come from the text. First write each sentence in note form, using arrows to show the direction of the causal relations. Then write a paraphrase of your notes, using one of the different ways of expressing causality listed in the table. A sample answer has been provided for the first example.

12   *Unit 1   Mind, Body, and Health*

1 When stress is encountered continually the body's reactions are more likely to be harmful than helpful to us.

> continual stress ⟶ harmful bodily reactions
>
> Continual stress may lead to harmful bodily reactions.

2 Workers who experience the greatest degree of job pressures have been found to be especially likely to suffer from a large number of diseases.

3 Ulcers are a common disorder among people who work in occupations that make heavy psychological demands.

4 Stress may also contribute to disease in less direct ways, by influencing moods and behavior.

Task 2 Summarizing

> **B**eing able to write a summary is an important skill. It shows that you have understood what is most important in a text. A summary is different from a paraphrase. When you paraphrase, you look at a small part of the text and rewrite it in your own words. When you summarize, you look at the whole text and reduce it to a few sentences (still using your own words, not the author's).
>
> The first sentence of a summary should express the overall message of the text. The remaining sentences should present the most important ideas in the text. A good summary need not include details or supporting evidence for the main ideas.

1➤ The sentences that follow provide a detailed summary of "Stress and Illness" in jumbled order. Number them in the correct order.

____ *a* Those who are going through a divorce, or people with stressful jobs, such as air-traffic controllers, are in particular danger.

____ *b* Stress may also indirectly affect your health, since people who are under stress often engage in activities that are harmful.

____ *c* Researchers have found that people who experience a great deal of stress in their daily lives or in their jobs are more likely to get sick.

____ *d* They may overeat or not eat enough, smoke too much, drink too much alcohol, and not sleep well.

____ *e* Such bodily reactions to stress can lead to illnesses ranging from the common cold, to headaches, arthritis, ulcers, and even cancer.

____ *f* Stress, it seems, can cause the immune system not to function well and can cause harmful reactions such as an increase in acidic secretions in the stomach.

2➤ The summary you created by reordering the six sentences contains too much detail. Find the three least important sentences and delete them. Write out the remaining three to produce a well-written, clear, and concise summary.

PREPARING TO READ

Predicting the content

> **T**rying to predict what information will be in a text before you read is a good habit. It motivates you to read the text carefully to find out if your predictions were correct.

Read the following situations (described in the text) and predict how the questions that accompany them will be answered in the text. Compare your answers in groups.

1 Imagine two young lawyers who are told on a Friday that they have only the weekend to prepare a report on a complex case. Their chances of promotion may depend on how well they do. One feels threatened and fears that she might fail. The other feels challenged and excited at the opportunity of proving her worth. Which lawyer do you think prepares a better report?

   a the lawyer who feels threatened and anxious

   b the lawyer who feels challenged and excited

2 Two rats are given exactly the same amount of electric shock. One rat is able to turn off the shock; the other can only be passive and must wait for the shock to stop. Which rat do you think has a worse physical reaction to the shock?

   a the rat that could turn off the electricity

   b the rat that was passive

3 Two rats are given exactly the same amount of electric shock. However, one rat hears a buzzer ten seconds before each shock, the other hears nothing. Which rat do you think has a worse physical reaction to the electric shock?

   a the rat who heard the buzzer before the shock

   b the rat who got no warning that the shock was coming

4 Sometimes the death of a loved one is expected, as after a long illness. In other cases it comes without warning. Which do you think is usually easier to cope with?

   a the expected death of a loved one

   b the sudden death of a loved one

5 Usually professors tell you when they are going to give a test or a quiz. It is scheduled for a particular day. But sometimes professors come into class and give surprise quizzes. Which do you think most students prefer?

   a scheduled quizzes

   b surprise quizzes

NOW READ

Now read the text "Coping With Stress." When you finish, turn to the tasks on page 17.

3   COPING WITH STRESS

It is Friday evening and two young lawyers get phone calls at home. The trial date for an important case has been moved up. Both of the lawyers will now have to prepare a report for the case by Monday morning. It is a threatening situation for both. Each must do extensive research and write a complex document of some forty pages all in a single weekend. *5* Furthermore, each knows that her work will be evaluated by the firm's partners, and how well she does may greatly influence her future in the firm. One of the lawyers finds the situation extremely stressful; she feels tremendous anxiety, experiences headaches and stomach upsets, and has difficulty working. She somehow manages to produce a report, but she *10* is not at all happy with it. The other lawyer, although she too feels the pressure of the situation, sees it not so much as a threat but as a challenge – an opportunity to show how good she is. She moves into the firm's offices for the weekend and, sleeping only three hours a night, completes a brilliant report with a clear mind and a surge of energy. *15*

As this example helps illustrate, stress is caused not so much by events themselves as by the ways in which people perceive and react to events. As the Greek philosopher Epicetus declared almost 2,000 years ago, "We are not disturbed by things, but our opinions about things." To cope with stress effectively, we often need to redefine the situation from one of *20* threat to one of challenge or opportunity.

DEGREE OF CONTROL

An important influence on people's ability to cope with stressful situations is the degree of control they feel they can exercise over the situation. Both animals and humans have been found to cope better with painful or threatening stimuli when they feel that they can exercise some degree *25* of control rather than being passive and helpless victims (Thompson, 1981). Such a sense of control can help minimize the negative consequences of stress, both psychological and physical. In one well-known experiment, Jay Weiss (1972) administered electric shocks to pairs of rats. In each pair, one of the two animals was given a degree of control over *30* the situation; it could reach through a hole in the cage and press a panel that would turn off the shock both for itself and for its partner. Thus, the two rats received exactly the same number of shocks, but one was passive and helpless, and the other was in control. After a continuous 21-hour session, the animals were sacrificed and their stomachs examined *35* for ulcers. Those rats who could exert control had much less ulceration than their helpless partners.

The ability to control painful stimuli often benefits humans, too. For example, the loud music coming from your stereo is probably not stressful; in fact, it's quite enjoyable. But the same music coming from the *40* place next door can be terribly irritating and stressful. Merely knowing that one can control a noise makes it less bothersome. That's one reason

By taping the lecture, this international student at an American university is taking control of a stressful situation.

Too little stress and too few challenges in one's life can also be unhealthy.

stress-resistant personality
type of person who feels in control, who welcomes change and challenge, and who copes well when facing stressful situations

why your blaring stereo does not bother you – you know you can always turn it off.

PREDICTABILITY

45 Even when you cannot control them, unpleasant events tend to be less stressful if they are predictable – if you at least know when they will occur. This was demonstrated by Weiss (1972) in another study with rats. One group of rats heard a buzzer about ten seconds before they would receive a shock; although the animals could not escape the shock, at least
50 they had a chance to prepare themselves for the expected pain. A second group of rats received no such warnings; the shocks came unpredictably. Weiss found that the rats who were forewarned of the shocks developed fewer ulcers than the rats who were not forewarned. This finding, too, has parallels in human life. The death of a loved one, for example, is usu-
55 ally less traumatic when it is anticipated than when it is unexpected. On a less tragic level, many students find surprise quizzes to be more upsetting than scheduled quizzes that they can prepare for.

PERSONALITY FACTORS

Are some people generally better than others at coping with stress? Recent research suggests that the answer is yes – that there is a certain
60 kind of person who has a relatively **stress-resistant personality**. Suzanne Kobasa (1982) has found that people who cope well with stress tend to be "committed" to what they are doing (rather than alienated), to feel in control (rather than powerless), and to welcome moderate amounts of change and challenge. In studies of people facing stressful situations,
65 Kobasa and her associates have found that those with stress-resistant personalities – that is, those who are high in commitment, control, and challenge – experience fewer physical illnesses than those whose personalities are less hardy.

Until recently it was generally believed that to maintain good health
70 people should strive to avoid stressors in their lives. Such a strategy can be quite limiting, however. The desire to avoid stress may also lead people to avoid potentially beneficial changes in their lives, such as job changes or promotions. Moreover, the attempt to avoid stress is often unrealistic. How, for example, can a person avoid such shocks as a par-
75 ent's death? In fact, if people do not confront a certain amount of stress in their lives, they will end up being bored and unstimulated, which can also be physically harmful. In the last analysis, each person needs to come to terms with stress in his or her own way, sometimes trying to avoid it, but sometimes accepting it or even seeking it out as a challenge
80 to be mastered.

AFTER YOU READ

Task 1 Reading for main ideas

> **U**nderstanding the main ideas and identifying the specific details used to support them is normally your primary task when reading a college text.

The following three main principles emerge from this text about how to cope with stress:

a The more control you have over a stressful event, the easier it is to cope with.
b The more you are able to predict a stressful event, the easier it is to cope with.
c The more you perceive a stressful event as a challenge rather than a threat, the easier it is to cope with.

Each of the five situations introduced in the "Preparing To Read" activity, "Predicting the Content," supports one of these three principles. Match each one to the principle that it illustrates.

_____ *1* The anxious lawyer and the excited lawyer
_____ *2* The active rat and the passive rat
_____ *3* The rat that hears the buzzer and the rat that hears nothing
_____ *4* The sudden death of a loved one and the expected death of a loved one
_____ *5* Scheduled quizzes and surprise quizzes

Task 2 Building vocabulary: Dealing with unknown words

> **I**t is important to develop effective strategies for dealing with the difficult or unfamiliar vocabulary that you are going to come across in your reading.

1➤ Work with a partner and make a list of at least five different strategies you can use when you come across a word that you do not know.

2➤ Now find the following "difficult" vocabulary in the text (verbs are given here as infinitives). Decide which strategy you would use (and why) for each one.

to sacrifice an animal (line 35)   to be committed (line 62)
to have ulceration (line 36)   to feel alienated (line 62)
to be bothersome (line 42)   to be hardy (line 68)
to be forewarned (line 52)   to strive to do something (line 70)
to have parallels (line 54)   to come to terms with (line 78)
to be traumatic (line 55)   to seek out challenge (line 79)

Task 3 Writing a summary

Write a summary of "Coping With Stress." Remember to include only the main ideas and to omit highly specific details or supporting evidence. Look back at Task 2 in the previous section to help you think about what to include in your summary.

PREPARING TO READ

How much do you already know?

> The more you already know about a topic, the easier it is to read new information on that topic. Asking yourself questions about the topic of a text before you read it will help you recall what you already know.

How much do you know about cancer? Discuss these questions with a partner or the class.

1 What is cancer? Which parts of the body are often attacked by cancer?
2 What are some examples of carcinogens (things that can cause cancer)?
3 What is the immune system? How does it function? What happens when the immune system is not functioning properly, for example, when someone has AIDS?
4 The author mentions a new field of study called *psychoimmunology*. Look at the parts of this word and guess what is studied in this field.
5 What relationships do you think scientists might find between depression and stress, and one's susceptibility to disease or one's ability to overcome it?

Building vocabulary: Learning word clusters

> If you know the words that cluster around a particular topic, you will find it much easier to read about that topic.

How well do you know the vocabulary associated with cancer? With a partner discuss the meanings of the words in bold. They are given within the clauses or sentences in which they occur in the text that you are about to read.

1 These . . . **malignant tumors** can proceed to invade bodily tissues and cause damage to the body's organs.
2 Another aspect of behavior that can affect the course of cancer is a person's efforts to help **detect cancer at an early stage**. . . .
3 In a study of women who underwent **mastectomy** for early stage breast cancer, . . .
4 These and other changes apparently make it harder for the immune system to **reject cancer cells**.
5 In another study, widowed husbands were found to have a decline in the function of their **white blood cells**. . . .

NOW READ

Now read the text "Psychology and Cancer." When you finish, turn to the tasks that begin on page 22.

4 PSYCHOLOGY AND CANCER

Cancer is the second leading cause of death in America. It remains one of the least understood diseases and, partly for that reason, one of the most feared. In cancer, cells of the body become altered and then multiply rapidly, creating clusters of cells whose growth is uncontrollable. These cell clusters, or malignant tumors, can proceed to invade bodily tissue and cause damage to the body's organs. In many cases, the eventual outcome is death.

Medical scientists are just beginning to understand the biological mechanisms of cell behavior that underlie the onset and development of cancer. But even though these mechanisms remain mysterious, it's clear that in several respects cancer can be linked to behavior. The likelihood of cancer can be greatly increased by exposure to certain substances in the environment, including cigarette smoke, asbestos, chemical wastes, and radiation. We cannot always control our own exposure to such *carcinogens* (cancer-causing agents), but in at least some instances we can. Another aspect of behavior that can affect the course of cancer is a person's efforts to help detect cancer at an early stage, when it is more likely to be treated successfully. That is why, for example, women are encouraged to examine their breasts regularly and to seek medical advice if they note any unusual changes.

Early detection of cancer makes it easier to treat successfully.

EMOTIONAL REACTIONS AND THE IMMUNE SYSTEM

There is also increasing evidence that people's emotions are involved in the progression of cancer once it has begun. In a study of women who underwent mastectomy for early-stage breast cancer, Steven Greer and his coworkers in England (Greer and Morris, 1981) found that women who reacted to their diagnosis with either a fighting spirit or strong denial were more likely to be free of disease eight years later than were women who reacted with stoic acceptance or with feelings of helplessness. Other recent research suggests that those women who complain most about their breast cancer – who express their anger outwardly, instead of keeping it inside – have a better chance for recovery (Levy, 1984).

Recent studies have begun to shed light on the biological mechanisms that may account for such links between emotions and cancer. These links involve the functioning of the body's immune system, a collection of billions of cells that travel through the bloodstream and defend the body against invasion by foreign agents, including bacteria and viruses, and against cells that become cancerous. Psychological factors can influence immune functioning, and the expanding field of research on their influences is called **psychoimmunology** (Borysenko, 1983). It is believed that small cancers form frequently in everyone but that our immune systems usually reject them. However, prolonged stress may lead to elevated levels of corticosteroids and to lower levels of the neurotransmitter

psychoimmunology
a field of study that investigates the effect of psychological factors on the immune system

norepinephrine in the brain. These and other changes apparently make it harder for the immune system to reject cancer cells. When the organism copes with the stress in an active way, these changes in the immune system seem to be minimized; when the organism reacts with helplessness and depression, the changes are maximized.

5   These links between stress, helplessness, immune function, and cancer have been demonstrated experimentally in studies with animals. In one study, Lawrence Sklar and Hymie Anisman (1979) injected three groups of mice with the same number of cancer cells. One group was then exposed to an electric shock that they could learn to escape by jumping over a barrier to safety. A second group was exposed to the same duration of shock but had no means of actively coping with the stress. The third group was never shocked. The cancer grew fastest and led to earliest death among the animals that had no means of coping with their stress. In contrast, the animals that could mount an effective escape did not differ in tumor growth from those that had not been shocked at all. Other studies have directly linked such inescapable stress to changes in the animal's immune system – for example, to a suppression of the proliferation of disease-fighting lymphocytes in the bloodstream (Laudenslager et al., 1983).

6   The link between stress, helplessness, and cancers has been demonstrated in humans as well. In one dramatic study, Richard Shekelle and his coworkers (1981) studied over 2,000 men who had taken a psychological test that diagnoses depression and other emotional states. Seventeen years later, the researcher found that those men who had been highly depressed at the time of the testing had twice the chance of dying of cancer as men who had not been depressed. Since depressed people might drink more alcohol or smoke more cigarettes, which might in turn increase the risk of cancer, Shekelle took this into account when he ana-

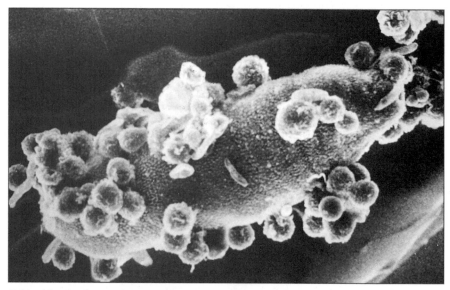

White blood cells attacking an invading microbe.

The death of a loved one may lead to depression, which is thought to increase one's risk of cancer.

lyzed his data; the association between depression and cancer still held, regardless of drinking or smoking rates. In another study, widowed husbands were found to have a decline in the function of their white blood cells – part of the immune system – within two months of their wives' deaths (Schiefler et al., 1980).

RECOMMENDATIONS FOR TREATMENT

Findings on the links between emotional reactions to stress and the pro- *7* gression of cancer have given rise to some recommendations for the treatment of cancer patients. In particular, programs that can help give cancer patients a greater feeling of control over their destinies and that can help them adopt a "fighting spirit" might just increase their odds. So far, however, there is no solid evidence that such programs can in fact extend people's lives (Levy, 1984). Developing programs that might have such an impact is an exciting frontier in health psychology.

AFTER YOU READ

Task 1 Scanning

Scan the text and locate the paragraphs in which the following studies are mentioned. Fill in the number of the paragraph in the blank.

_____ *a* Schiefler et al.   _____ *d* Greer and Morris
_____ *b* Laudenslager et al.   _____ *e* Shekelle
_____ *c* Sklar and Anisman   _____ *f* Levy

Task 2 Reading for detail

Match the researchers on the left with their findings (in note form) on the right.

___ *1* Schiefler et al.

___ *2* Greer and Morris

___ *3* Laudenslager et al.

___ *4* Shekelle

___ *5* Sklar and Anisman

___ *6* Levy

a expressing anger ⟶ better chance of cancer recovery

b death of wife ⟶ white blood cells function less effectively

c helplessness in mice ⟶ faster growing cancer

d helplessness in animals ⟶ fewer lymphocytes in the blood

e depression ⟶ increased chance of dying of cancer

f showing fighting spirit ⟶ better chance of cancer recovery

Task 3 Citing studies in your writing

> In an essay or an examination answer, you may want to cite (refer to) a study you have read about. To do so, you should include the following:
>
> *1* research subject area
> *2* researchers' names
> *3* year (usually of publication of the research)
> *4* the research finding
>
> To cite a study in your writing, you can use the following sentence pattern:
>
> *In a study of 1, 2 (3) found that 4.*

Study this sentence, which cites the work of Schiefler et al. described in the text.

In a study of [1]widowed husbands, [2]Schiefler et al. [3](1980) found that [4]within two months after the deaths of their wives, these men's white blood cells functioned less effectively .

Now cite the other five studies described in this text in the same way. In reporting the findings, paraphrase them using your own words. Do not copy word for word from the text.

1 Greer and Morris

2 Laudenslager et al.

3 Shekelle

4 Sklar and Anisman

5 Levy

CHAPTER 1 Writing assignment

Choose one of the following topics as your chapter writing assignment.

1 Describe some stressful event in your life. Did you cope well with the stress? What could you have done differently? Was your physical health affected by this stress?

2 Imagine a friend of yours has either just entered college or is about to enter college. What advice would you give your friend to help him or her cope with the stress of college? (If you are studying at a college in the United States, imagine your friend is about to join you at the same school.)

3 Much of this chapter examines the question of whether mental states can influence physical health. What evidence do you find for the idea that the mind does influence the body? Refer to evidence in the chapter and your own knowledge, experience, and beliefs.

PREPARING TO READ

Personalizing the topic

> Thinking about your personal connections to a topic before you read about it will help you absorb new information on that topic.

Fill out this questionnaire. After you read the text, look at your answers to see if you are at risk for heart disease.

Are You at Risk?	Yes	No
1 Are you male?	☐	☐
2 Do you smoke?	☐	☐
3 Are you overweight?	☐	☐
4 Does/did your mother or father have heart disease?	☐	☐
5 Are you a competitive person? Do you always want to win or be the best at everything?	☐	☐
6 Do you often feel that you never have enough time to do all the things you want or have to do?	☐	☐
7 Do you hide what you are really feeling?	☐	☐

Skimming for main ideas

> Skimming means reading only small parts of a text, such as the beginnings and ends of paragraphs, in order to get an overview of the organization of the text and its main ideas. Skimming a text is an excellent prereading habit. When you do a close reading of the text after skimming it, you will find that you read more fluently and accurately.

Skim through the text and find the paragraph that deals with each of the following topics. Write the number of the paragraph in the blank.

_____ a Causes of heart disease
_____ b Programs to help Type A personalities relax more
_____ c Differences between Type A and Type B personalities
_____ d Statistics about the death rate from heart disease
_____ e Reasons why Type A personalities are more susceptible to heart disease
_____ f Differences in heart disease rate for men and women

NOW READ

Now read the text "Heart Disease." When you finish, look back at your answers to the questionnaire in "Personalizing the Topic" and decide whether you are at risk for heart disease. Then turn to the tasks that begin on page 28.

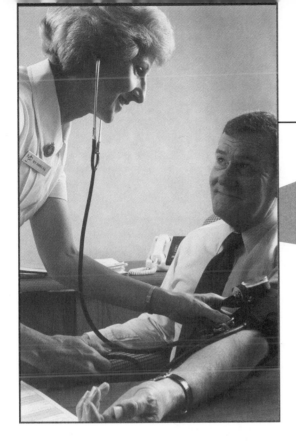

1 HEART DISEASE

Heart disease is Western society's number-one killer. It accounts for one-third of all deaths in America and for well over half the deaths among middle-age men. Heart disease was relatively rare in America at the turn of the century, but it has risen dramatically since then, with a slight downturn since 1960. Heart disease is often viewed as a disease of modern living, spurred on by the habits and the stress of industrialized society. Evidence for this idea comes from the fact that non-Western societies have relatively low rates of heart disease. And there is a higher rate of heart disease among immigrants to America, such as Japanese-Americans and Chinese-Americans, than among those who remain in their native country, suggesting that something about the Western environment promotes the development of the disease (Shapiro, 1983). [1]

Heart disease usually involves the formation of a fatty substance called *plaque* in the walls of the coronary arteries that supply blood to the heart. If the arteries become narrowed enough or blocked, the person may suffer a heart attack (death of a region of heart muscle tissue). Among the many factors that have been found to be related to the risk of developing heart disease are high blood pressure (or *hypertension*), a history of heart disease among one's close relatives (indicating a possible genetic predisposition to the disease), cigarette smoking, being relatively overweight, and a high level of a fatty substance called *cholesterol* in the blood. In addition to all of these well-established risk factors, it is now clear that stress can have a major impact on the development of [2] heart disease. People who continually undergo a great deal of stress – and who lack the ability to control it – are at a significantly greater risk for heart disease than people who undergo less stress or who can manage stress successfully. Jobs that impose high psychological demands but that provide the worker with little control – such as a cook, waiter, and hospital orderly – seem to breed heart disease (Karasek, 1981).

THE TYPE A BEHAVIOR PATTERN

3 Whereas some jobs may make heavier psychological demands than others, certain sorts of people, regardless of their occupation, seem to make heavy psychological demands on themselves – and, as a result, run a greater risk of heart disease. People with a particular personality style, called the *coronary-prone behavior pattern* and commonly labeled **Type A**, have been found to be especially susceptible to heart disease (Friedman and Rosenman, 1974). Type A people are hard-driving, competitive, and aggressive. They experience great time urgency, always trying to do more and more in less and less time. People who have an opposite sort of personality are termed **Type B**. Others are categorized somewhere in between.

4 Many studies have confirmed that Type A people are more susceptible to heart disease than Type B people (Dembroski et al., 1984). One probable reason is that Type A people tend to make greater demands on themselves and to expose themselves to more stressful situations than do Type B people. One study of college football players found, for example, that Type A players were rated by their coaches as playing harder than Type B players when they were injured (Carver, DeGregorio, and Gillis, 1981). Type A people also tend to have an unusually intense physiological reaction to the stress that they encounter. When they are faced with a challenging situation, they tend to manifest higher blood pressure and greater increases in heart rate and in the level of epinephrine in their blood than Type B people. Some researchers believe that this greater physiological reactivity under stress – sometimes called *hot reactivity* – is the key to the link between the Type A pattern and heart disease (Dembroski et al., 1984).

5 The bulk of the research on psychological factors in heart disease has focused on men rather than women. Even among women who face highly stressful situations, whether at work or at home, the risk of heart disease remains considerably lower than for men. Many biological and psychological factors may contribute to this difference. Among them is the consistent finding that although women tend to express their emotions more openly than men do, their physiological reactions to stress tend to be less intense (Frankenheuser, 1983). In terms of the risk of heart disease, then, it may be better to let one's emotions show outwardly than to bury them inside, where they may eventually cause damage to one's body.

6 Because of the links between the Type A behavior pattern and heart disease, various approaches have been taken to changing this pattern of

Type A
used to describe people who are hard-driving, competitive, aggressive

Type B
used to describe people who are easy-going, noncompetitive, unaggressive

The Type A personality finds it difficult to relax.

Women may reduce their risk of heart disease by talking openly about their emotions.

behavior. For example, Type A people have been taught relaxation exercises and other techniques to manage stress. They have been encouraged to develop nonstressful hobbies and they have been given therapy sessions to help change their pressured view of the world. Some programs have had a degree of success in altering the behavioral and psychological reaction of Type A individuals (Suinn, 1982). So far, however, the success has been limited. The Type A pattern seems to be learned over the course of many years, and it is supported by the competitive, achievement-oriented aspects of Western society. As such, it is not a simple matter to change this pattern. Indeed, as Joan Borysenko (1984) notes, "One of the most stressful things for a Type A is to be told to relax."

AFTER YOU READ

Task 1   Test-taking: Answering true/false questions about a text

True/false questions are fairly common in college tests. Read this list of strategies for answering them.

- Answer every question. You always have a 50/50 chance of being right.
- Pay special attention to statements with negatives in them. These are often tricky to answer. Remember that a negative statement that is correct is true.
- Pay attention to words like *always* or *never* or *all*. Statements that are very "black or white" tend to be false. On the other hand, more tentative "gray" statements are more likely to be true.
- Read all parts of a statement carefully. Some parts may be true, but if any one part of it is false, then the whole statement is false.
- In any series of true/false questions, there is usually about the same number of true statements as false ones.

Decide if the following statements are true (T) or false (F), according to the information in this text.

_____ 1   More than fifty percent of all deaths in the United States are from heart disease.

_____ 2   When people emigrate to the United States from non-Western countries, they are more likely to suffer from heart disease than if they had stayed in their original homelands.

_____ 3   If one's close relatives have had heart disease, this is a possible indication that you may eventually suffer from heart disease.

_____ 4   Research has established that for some people there is a relationship between the degree of stress in their life and the risk of developing heart disease.

_____ 5   Two men doing exactly the same job are equally likely to develop heart disease.

_____ 6   Type A people tend to have aggressive and unrelaxed personalities; however, they are better able to manage stress effectively and are less likely to develop heart disease than Type B people.

_____ 7   Only one researcher has ever found that Type A people are more susceptible to heart disease than Type B people.

_____ 8   When Type A people experience stress, they tend to have a higher heart rate and higher blood pressure than Type B people.

_____ 9   When a Type A man and a Type A woman do the same job and receive the same amount of stress, they have an equal chance of developing heart disease.

_____ 10 Most programs trying to change the behavior of Type A people have not been very successful.

Task 2 Language focus: Making comparisons

In this text, a number of comparisons are made. For example, Type A people are compared to Type B people, and men are compared to women. These comparisons can be made by using comparative adjectives, which can occur in the following structures:

1 ADJ + *-er* + *than* (used with adjectives of one syllable)

2 *more* + ADJ + *than* (used with adjectives of three syllables or more*)

3 *less* + ADJ + *than* (used with most adjectives)

4 *not as* + ADJ + *as* (used with any adjective)

1► For each adjective, write two sentences comparing Type A and Type B people. Start your first sentence by referring to Type A people and the second by referring to Type B.

1 aggressive

> a. Type A people are more aggressive than Type B people.
>
> b. Type B people are less aggressive than Type A people.
>   (or Type B people are not as aggressive as Type A people)

2 competitive

3 laid-back

4 good at controlling their emotions

5 achievement-oriented

6 calm

2► Many of the comparisons made in this text involve this structure:

comparative adjective + noun + *than*

Make comparisons between Type A and Type B people in terms of each of the categories listed.

1 the psychological demands they make upon themselves

> Type A people make greater psychological demands upon themselves than Type B people.

2 their risk of having high blood pressure

3 their heart disease rate

4 their sense of time urgency

5 their reaction to difficult situations

Task 3 Writing a paragraph

Write a paragraph contrasting Type A personality types with Type B personality types.

---

*Two-syllable adjectives may act like one-syllable adjectives, for example, *happy/happier;* or like three-syllable adjectives, for example, *useful/more useful.*

PREPARING TO READ

Thinking about the topic

Work with a partner and discuss the following topics.

The ill effects of smoking

1 In what ways is cigarette smoking bad for the health of the smoker?

2 Are there laws against smoking in public places in your country? Why do such laws exist?

Starting and quitting smoking

3 The author states that many people start smoking because of "pressure from peers." What is peer pressure? How do you think it might cause people to start smoking?

4 The author states that addiction to cigarettes is in part physiological and in part psychological. What do you think is meant by this?

Preventing smoking

5 At what age is it legal to buy a pack of cigarettes in your country? Do you think it is too easy for young people to buy cigarettes? What could be done?

6 Are there warnings on packs of cigarettes in your country? What do they say? What else could the government do to discourage smoking?

Skimming for main ideas

Skim through the text and write in the number of the paragraph that deals with each of the following topics.

_____ a Methods used to get people to quit smoking
_____ b Future prospects for the popularity of smoking
_____ c Statistics about smoking and its ill effects
_____ d Smoking prevention programs
_____ e The failure rate of stop-smoking programs
_____ f Reasons why people start and continue to smoke

NOW READ

Now read the text "Smoking." When you finish, turn to the tasks that begin on page 34.

2 SMOKING

In 1964, the Surgeon General of the United States issued a famous report 1
concluding that cigarette smoke is a direct cause of lung cancer. And
since 1966, every pack of cigarettes in the United States has carried a
health warning. More recently, the major role of smoking in causing
heart disease has been firmly established. Smoking has been conclusive-
ly linked to many other diseases as well, including bronchitis, emphyse-
ma, larynx cancer, and pancreatic cancer. There is also mounting evidence that simply being exposed to other people's smoke increases the
risk of lung disease, especially in children. Despite these deadly effects,
however, about 35 percent of adult men and 25 percent of adult women
in the United States smoke cigarettes, averaging one and a half packs a
day for a national grand total of some 600 billion packs a year (U.S.
Department of Health and Human Services, 1981). Because cigarette
smoking is generally viewed as the most important behavioral risk to
health, it has become a central concern of health psychologists.

Given the general knowledge of the health risks of smoking, it is no 2
wonder that the majority of smokers have tried at some time in their lives
to quit. But in most cases their attempts have been unsuccessful. People
begin smoking, often when they are adolescents, for a variety of reasons,
including the example of parents and pressure from peers. If others in
one's group of friends are starting to smoke, it can be hard to resist going
along with the crowd. Once people start smoking, they are likely to get
hooked. The addiction to smoking is partly physiological; smokers
become used to the effects of nicotine and experience painful withdraw-
al symptoms when they give it up. In addition, people become psychologically dependent on smoking as a way of reducing anxiety and cop-

*Young people often start smoking when they see their friends smoking – pressure from
peers may be hard to resist.*

One technique for quitting smoking involves stimulus control – if he wants to quit smoking, this smoker may also have to give up his after-dinner coffee.

ing with particular situations. Because of these physiological and psychological forces, quitting is difficult and the relapse rate is high.

3   Psychologists have developed a variety of behavior modification techniques to help people stop smoking. In the *rapid smoking technique*, smokers in a clinic or lab are asked to smoke continually, puffing every six to eight seconds, until they can't tolerate it any longer. This technique is an example of a form of classical conditioning called *aversive conditioning*. Making smoking a painful (or aversive) rather than a pleasant experience can create a conditioned aversion in the smoker, motivating her to avoid smoking even when she leaves the clinic. Smoking cessation programs also commonly teach people techniques of *stimulus control*, in which smokers learn first to become aware of the stimuli and situations that commonly lead to smoking, and then to avoid these situations or to develop alternative behaviors. If you find, for example, that you usually smoke while drinking an after-dinner cup of coffee, you might do well to give up coffee and take an invigorating, smokeless after-dinner walk instead.

4   Programs that include such techniques often help people stop smoking for a period of weeks or months. The problem is that within six months to a year 80 to 85 percent of the "quitters" return to their smoky ways (Lichtenstein, 1982). One factor that often seems to help a reformed smoker stay off cigarettes is the encouragement and support of a spouse or other close family members or friends (Ockene et al., 1982). There is reason to believe that a large proportion of smokers can quit for good if they are strongly motivated to do so (Schacter, 1982). But the fact remains that so far there is no program that can consistently enable people to stay off the weed.

The difficulty of quitting emphasizes the importance of preventing 5
cigarette smoking by young people. Various sorts of smoking prevention
programs have been attempted, often in junior high schools.
Traditionally, these efforts have focused on explaining the long-term
health risks of smoking. But people often have the knack of putting such
gloomy long-term warnings out of their minds, and these programs have
been notably ineffective. More recently, Richard Evans and his coworkers (1981) have emphasized teaching children and adolescents how to
resist the social pressures that often lead young people to try smoking.
For example, students are shown videotapes of a situation in which an
adolescent is offered a cigarette by a friend but turns down the offer. The
students are then given the opportunity to practice, or role-play, the
behavior of refusing a cigarette. Such training helps prepare the 12- or 13-
year-old to deal effectively with similar social influence situations in real
life and seems to have been successful in influencing students in the
direction of deciding not to smoke.

A total solution to our society's smoking problem will not come, how- 6
ever, until society's expectations change in a major way; that is, until
smoking is no longer viewed as a "grown-up" or approved thing to do.
Such a change has begun to take place in recent years and there have
been significant reductions in the numbers of smokers in America. More
smokers have been quitting and fewer young people have been deciding
to take up smoking in the first place.

AFTER YOU READ

Task 1 *Analyzing paragraph organization*

> **U**nderstanding how paragraphs are organized can help you read more effectively. The most basic type of paragraph organization is a *listing paragraph*, which usually starts with a general statement followed by a list. Typically, the general statement indicates how many reasons/factors/characteristics/kinds there are, with either a specific number like *four* or a term like *a variety of*. Then the rest of the paragraph describes some or all of these reasons.

Analyze paragraphs 2, 3, and 5 of this text, which are listing paragraphs, and complete the partial outline given for each one.

Paragraph 2: Reasons why people start and cannot stop smoking

   a reasons for starting: peer pressure

   b reason cannot stop 1: _____

   c reason cannot stop 2: _____

Paragraph 3: _____

   a technique 1: _____

   b technique 2: stimulus control

Paragraph 5: Smoking prevention programs

   a program type 1: explanation of risks

   b program type 2: _____

Task 2 Writing a listing paragraph

A common way for a listing paragraph to begin is with sentences such as:

There are two/three/four reasons/factors/characteristics/kinds of . . .

There are a large number of different reasons/factors/characteristics/kinds of . . .

There are several reasons/factors/characteristics/kinds of . . .

There are various different reasons/factors/characteristics/kinds of . . .

If the list contains only two items, the sentences that follow may continue in this way:

One reason/factor/characteristic . . . The other . . .

If the list contains more than two items, the following sentences may continue in this way:

One reason/factor/characteristic . . . Another . . . A third . . . (and so on)

Choose one of the three paragraph outlines that you completed in Task 1. Working from the outline only, write the paragraph using your own words. Begin the paragraph with a listing-type topic sentence.

Task 3 Dramatizing the text

An effective way to determine if you have understood new information is to make use of that information in role play.

Work with a partner and choose one of the following situations related to the text on smoking. Prepare a role play and then act it out in front of the class.

1➤ One person plays a teenager refusing a cigarette; the other person is offering the cigarette and trying to insist that the teenager accept the cigarette. (Role-playing this situation is described in the text as an activity used in a program to help students stay away from smoking.)

2➤ One person is a teenager who has just started to smoke. The other person is the teenager's parent who strongly suspects that his or her child is beginning to smoke. Role-play a conversation in which the parent tries to convince the child not to take up smoking.

Task 4 Language focus: Awareness of levels of formality

Mostly textbooks are written in a formal style of English. However, occasionally authors will try to make their language seem more friendly by including *colloquial* or less formal language. Which words does the author use in this text to reduce the formality of the language?

1 In paragraphs 2 and 4, _____ is used instead of *give up*.
2 In paragraph 2, _____ is used instead of *to get addicted*.
3 In paragraph 4, _____ is used instead of *tobacco*.
4 In paragraph 4, _____ is used instead of *people who have given up*.
5 In paragraph 5, _____ is used instead of *have a special ability to do something*.

PREPARING TO READ

Thinking about the topic

Discuss the answers to the following questions with a partner.

1 What are the most popular sports shown on TV in your country?
2 What is aerobic exercise?
3 What fitness activities are popular in your country? Are there health clubs? Do people work out on machines? Is bodybuilding popular? (For men or women or both?) Is jogging popular?
4 What are some of the benefits of exercise?
5 Why do so many people do little or no regular exercise?

Speed reading

> In college, students are often given very large reading assignments. They do not have the time to read these very slowly and carefully. Instead they have to develop a fast reading style known as speed reading. To practice your speed reading use the following techniques.
>
> **Techniques for speed reading**
>
> - Do not vocalize, that is, say the words under your breath as you read.
> - Do not run your finger or a pencil beneath the words as you read.
> - Try to focus on groups of words, not individual words.
> - Try not to backtrack over the text.
> - Guess at the general meaning of words you are not sure about.
> - Skip over words that you have no idea about and that do not seem too important.
> - Slow down slightly for key information, such as definitions and main ideas.
> - Speed up for less important information, such as examples and unimportant details.

NOW READ

Now read the text "Exercise." Practice the speed-reading techniques. Time yourself (or your teacher will time you). When you finish, make a note of how long it took you to read the whole text. Then turn to the tasks that begin on page 40.

3 EXERCISE

In recent decades, large numbers of Americans have led physically inactive lives. People shuffle out to their cars in the morning, sit or stand in one place most of the day, ride home, and settle into easy chairs to watch other people play baseball or football on television. In the process, people get little vigorous exercise. Today, however, more and more people are jogging, swimming, bicycling, and engaging in other forms of *aerobic exercise* – exercise that requires a constant flow of oxygen. The exercise boom is a good example of how general social values and expectations affect health-related behaviors. There were few joggers twenty years ago, but there are millions today.

HEALTH BENEFITS OF EXERCISE

The health benefits of aerobic exercise are not as obvious as the health risks of cigarette smoking. Nevertheless, people who lead sedentary lives, without much exercise, have been found to be at greater risk for heart disease and other illnesses. Researchers at Harvard and Stanford recently reported the results of a major study of 17,000 middle-age and older men who were first studied as college students between 1926 and 1950 and then followed up periodically for many decades (Paffenberger et al., 1984). The researchers found that those men who exercised regularly, even at moderate levels, lived longer than those who did not. Even after correcting for such factors as family history, the death rate due to heart disease of the least active group was almost twice as high as that

People today are more aware than ever of the importance of regular exercise.

RECOMMENDED WEIGHT TABLES*

Men

Height in feet and inches	Ideal weight range in pounds, depending on height and frame size		
	Small	Medium	Large
5' 2"	128-134	131-141	138-150
5' 3"	130-136	133-143	140-153
5' 4"	132-138	135-145	142-156
5' 5"	134-140	137-148	144-160
5' 6"	136-142	139-151	146-164
5' 7"	138-145	142-154	149-168
5' 8"	140-148	145-157	152-172
5' 9"	142-151	148-160	155-176
5' 10"	144-154	151-163	158-180
5' 11"	146-157	154-166	161-184
6' 0"	149-160	157-170	164-188
6' 1"	152-164	160-174	168-192
6' 2"	155-168	164-178	172-197
6' 3"	158-172	167-182	176-202
6' 4"	162-176	171-187	181-207

Women

Height in feet and inches	Ideal weight range in pounds, depending on height and frame size		
	Small	Medium	Large
4' 10"	102-111	109-121	118-131
4' 11"	103-113	111-123	120-134
5' 0"	104-115	113-126	122-137
5' 1"	106-118	115-129	125-140
5' 2"	108-121	118-132	128-143
5' 3"	111-124	121-135	131-147
5' 4"	114-127	124-138	134-151
5' 5"	117-130	127-141	137-155
5' 6"	120-133	130-144	140-159
5' 7"	123-136	133-147	143-163
5' 8"	126-139	136-150	146-167
5' 9"	129-142	139-153	149-170
5' 10"	132-145	142-156	152-173
5' 11"	135-148	145-159	155-176
6' 0"	138-151	148-162	158-179

*Adapted from MetLife Height and Weight Tables, Metropolitan Life Insurance Company

Exercise can help you achieve your recommended weight.

for the most active group. Another recent study found that both men and women who kept physically fit were much less likely to develop high blood pressure (a common precursor of heart disease) than those who did not keep fit (Blair et al., 1984).

Exercise may reduce the risk of heart disease and other diseases in several ways. First, there is evidence that regular exercise can favorably alter blood levels of different forms of cholesterol, which in turn may be related to the likelihood of plaque forming in coronary arteries (Wood and Haskell, 1979). Second, exercise can improve the health of overweight people by helping them to lose weight. Third, exercise often has psychological benefits, helping to relieve depression (McCann and Holmes, 1984) and increasing people's general sense of well-being (Folkins and Sime, 1981). These psychological benefits can, in turn, make people better able to cope with stress and to engage in other health-producing behaviors, such as cutting down on smoking and drinking.

EXERCISE PROGRAMS

Despite the physical fitness boom, a large proportion of Americans still fail to exercise regularly. In particular, people who begin exercise programs because of an identified health risk are as likely as not to drop out within three to six months (Martin and Dubbert, 1982). Thus, psychologists have been trying to develop exercise programs that will keep people exercising. As in the case of smoking cessation programs, the encouragement and support of spouses have been found to play a major role in keeping people from dropping out of exercise programs (Andrew et al., 1981). In addition, people are more likely to continue exercising when they are in a group rather than individual programs (Martin and Dubbert, 1982). Finally, people are more likely to adhere to a fitness program if they can incorporate the exercise into their daily lives – for example, by walking instead of driving short distances, or by walking up and down a few flights of stairs instead of taking the elevator. Because no special places, equipment, or times are needed, long-term adherence becomes more likely.

People often quit an exercise program unless they participate in a group or get some support from their spouse.

AFTER YOU READ

Time it took to read the text: _____ (to the nearest tenth of a minute, for example, 3.4 minutes).

Task 1 Reading for detail

Test your understanding of this text by answering these multiple-choice reading comprehension questions without looking back at the text. Choose the best answer from the choices listed.

1 Twenty years ago, a large number of Americans _____.
   a were physically inactive
   b used to go jogging
   c used to play sports, such as basketball, after work

2 How many men were involved in the Harvard and Stanford study?
   a 1,700
   b 17,000
   c 170,000

3 The Harvard and Stanford study showed that the men who were the least active increased their chance of dying from heart disease by _____.
   a 25 percent
   b 50 percent
   c 100 percent

4 People who exercise regularly have _____ people who do not keep fit.
   a lower blood pressure than
   b higher blood pressure than
   c the same level of blood pressure as

5 The author mentions three positive effects of exercise: reduction of blood cholesterol levels, reduction of weight, and _____.
   a increase in lung capacity
   b increase in general sense of well-being
   c reduction in chance of getting cancer

6 One of the side effects of exercising is that it makes you feel more positive about yourself and thus you are more likely to _____.
   a slowly increase the amount of stressful activities in your life
   b take good care of your body in other ways
   c seek professional help to deal with any mental problems like depression

7 Psychologists have played a role in the fitness boom by _____.

   a designing workout equipment that is interesting and enjoyable to use

   b advising people on which types of exercise to do

   c developing programs that keep people exercising

8 People are more likely to stay in an exercise program if they receive support and encouragement from their _____.

   a colleagues at work

   b psychologist

   c husband or wife

9 People are more likely to stay in an exercise program if they participate _____.

   a in a group

   b alone

   c with a friend

10 You are more likely to incorporate exercise into your life if you _____.

   a join a gym, go regularly, and get into the routine of doing the same exercises each visit

   b buy exercise equipment and work out at home

   c find natural ways during the day to do exercise, for example, take the stairs or walk instead of drive

Follow-up: How well did you read?

1➤ Reread the text and check your answers to the reading comprehension questions.

2➤ Fill in the box to calculate your reading speed in words per minute (wpm) and your percent correct on the reading comprehension questions. A good goal would be to read at about 250 wpm with an accuracy of 70 percent.

a time to read_____
b number of words_____590_____
c wpm (*b/a*)_____
d number correct_____
e percent correct (*d* x 10)_____

Task 2 Writing a summary

Read through the text again and then write a one-paragraph summary. Remember to include only the most important information.

PREPARING TO READ

Thinking about the topic

1▶ Write a list of at least ten behaviors that one should practice (or avoid) in order to be as healthy as possible. Review your list and choose the six most important items.

2▶ Form a group with other members of your class and compare your list with theirs. Then create a group list of healthy behaviors by choosing what you think are the *six* most important items from all of your lists.

3▶ Find out who is the healthiest person in your group, in other words, who practices the most of those six behaviors.

4▶ Compare your group's list with the lists of the other groups in the class. Decide which are the six most important items from all the lists.

5▶ Find out who is the healthiest person in the class!

Healthy Behaviors

1 _____

2 _____

3 _____

4 _____

5 _____

6 _____

7 _____

8 _____

9 _____

10 _____

NOW READ

Now read the text "Wellness." When you finish, turn to the tasks on page 44.

4 WELLNESS

As we have seen, the focus of medical care in our society has been shifting from curing disease to preventing disease – especially in terms of changing our many unhealthful behaviors, such as poor eating habits, smoking, and failure to exercise. The line of thought involved in this shift from curing to preventing can be pursued further. Imagine a person who is about the right weight, but does not eat very nutritious foods, who feels OK but exercises only occasionally, who goes to work every day, but is not an outstanding worker, who drinks a few beers at home most nights but does not drive while intoxicated, and who has no tumors or chest pains or abnormal blood counts, but sleeps a lot and often feels tired. This person is not ill. He or she may not even be at risk for any particular disease. But we can imagine that this person could be a lot healthier.

The field of medicine has not traditionally distinguished between someone who is merely "not ill" and someone who is in excellent health and paying attention to the body's special needs. Both types have simply been called "well." In recent years, however, some health practitioners have begun to apply the terms *well* and *wellness* only to those people who are actively striving to maintain and improve their health. People who are well are concerned with nutrition and exercise, and they make a point of monitoring their body's condition – for example, through regular breast self-examinations or blood pressure check-ups. Most important, perhaps, people who are well take active responsibility for all matters pertaining to their health. Even people who have a physical disease or handicap may be "well," in this new sense, if they make an effort to maintain the best possible health they can in the face of their physical limitations. "Wellness" may perhaps best be viewed not as a state that people can achieve, but as an ideal that people can strive for.

Unfortunately, as M. Robin DiMatteo and Howard Friedman (1982) note, wellness is sometimes viewed as a crazy new fad or as some sort of mystical road to truth and self-fulfillment. In fact, wellness is a sensible antidote to the narrow view that health involves the "fixing" of a passive, diseased body. People who are well are likely to be better able to resist disease and to fight disease when it strikes. And by focusing attention on healthy ways of living, the concept of wellness can have a beneficial impact on the ways in which people face the challenges of daily life.

According to this man's doctor he is not ill; but is he well?

AFTER YOU READ

Asking clarification questions about a text

> **I**t is important to be able to ask questions when you are not sure about the meaning of something in the text you are reading. In some college classes you are asked to take part in "lab" sessions. These are small discussion groups (usually 12 to 18 people) in which difficult concepts and texts can be discussed. The leader of the discussion is usually a graduate student, rather than the professor.

1➤ Here are some ways of asking for clarification about parts of this text. Notice the different ways in which the requests for clarification are phrased.

1 *I'm not sure I understand what the author means when he says that* there has been a shift "from curing disease to preventing disease." (1st paragraph)

2 *I don't think I quite understand what the author is saying when he says that* there can be a difference between someone who is "not ill" and someone who is well. (2nd paragraph)

3 *Could you give me examples of what the author means when he says that* people who are well are "monitoring their body's condition"? (2nd paragraph)

4 *Could you explain what the author means when he says that* it is possible for someone who has a physical disease or handicap to be "well"? (2nd paragraph)

5 *Could you give examples of what the author means by* "a crazy new fad" and a "mystical road to truth and self-fulfillment"? (3rd paragraph)

2➤ Work with a partner. Take turns role-playing a student making the above requests for clarification and the discussion leader who answers them.

CHAPTER 2 Writing assignment

Choose one of the following topics as your chapter writing assignment.

1 What can a person do to reduce the chances of getting heart disease?

2 Discuss the dangers of smoking and the benefits of exercise.

3 A psychologist can play an important role in the field of health care. Illustrate this statement, citing examples described in the chapter.

Development Through Life

In this unit we look at stages of human development after child-hood. In Chapter 3, we read about adolescence, often a stressful period, when the individual moves from dependent child toward independent adult. Then, in Chapter 4, we see how adult life can be divided into three stages, and learn about the different challenges, problems, and joys of each one.

PREVIEWING THE UNIT

> **B**efore reading a unit (or chapter) of a textbook, it is a good idea to preview the contents page and think about the topics that will be covered. This will give you an overview of how the whole unit is organized and what it is going to be about.

Read the contents page for Unit 2 and answer the following questions with a partner.

Chapter 3: Adolescence

1➤ Adolescence is the period between childhood and adulthood. It is described in the first section of this chapter as "a period of transition" and "filled with discovery, turmoil, growth toward independence." Discuss the following questions.

   1 What events mark the beginning of adolescence? In other words, when does childhood end?

   2 What events mark the end of this period? In other words, when does early adulthood begin?

   3 Based on your discussion of questions 1 and 2, what age range would you give to adolescence?

2➤ Tragically, many young people cannot cope with the difficulties of adolescence and take their own lives. The final section of Chapter 3 deals with this issue. With your partner make a list of possible causes of teenage suicide.

Chapter 4: Adulthood

1➤ In Chapter 4, adulthood is divided into three periods. The first two are called *early* and *middle adulthood*. Discuss the following questions.

   1 What are some of the most typical events in people's lives during these two periods of adulthood?

   2 What ages do you typically associate with these periods? Fill in the box.

early adulthood:	from ____ to ____ years old
middle adulthood:	from ____ to ____ years old

2➤ The last section of Chapter 4 deals with *late adulthood*. Why do you think many people have a hard time adjusting to the change from middle to late adulthood?

UNIT CONTENTS

PREPARING TO READ

Personalizing the topic

In the United States there is a stereotype of the adolescent. It is someone who has many problems, is often rebellious, and does not communicate well with his or her parents. To what extent is/was your adolescence like this? Respond to the following statements on a scale of 1 to 5. If you agree strongly, circle 1; if you disagree strongly, circle 5. Compare answers with your classmates.

During my adolescence I was/have been . . .	Strongly agree		Neutral		Strongly disagree
a very rebellious	1	2	3	4	5
b often in conflict with my parents	1	2	3	4	5
c full of negative thoughts about life	1	2	3	4	5
d under a great deal of stress	1	2	3	4	5

NOW READ

Now read the text "Defining Adolescence." When you finish, turn to the tasks on page 51.

"Hey, just because I live here doesn't mean I have to talk to you!"

CHAPTER 3

Adolescence

1 DEFINING ADOLESCENCE

The period of development that we call **adolescence** is an exciting one. It is filled with discovery, turmoil, growth toward independence, and the beginning of lifelong commitments. It is clearly a period of transition – from the dependence of childhood to the independence of adulthood. It is very difficult, however, to specify exactly when adolescence begins or when it ends.

   We may choose to define adolescence in biological terms. In that case, adolescence begins with the onset of *puberty* (with sexual maturity and a readiness to reproduce) and ends with the end of physical growth. Or we may adopt a more psychological perspective and emphasize the development of the cognitions, feelings, and behaviors that characterize adolescence. This approach views adolescence "as a psychological process occurring within the individual" (Forisha-Koviach, 1983). Additionally, it is also possible to think about adolescence from a social perspective by examining the role of adolescents in society. Such views generally define adolescence in terms of being in-between – not yet an adult, but no longer a child. In this context, the period usually lasts from the early teen years through one's highest level of education, when the individual is thought to enter the adult world.

   Actually, whether we accept a biological, psychological, or social approach to defining adolescence, we usually are talking about people between the ages of approximately 12 and 20. Some psychologists consider this period in terms of growth and positive change, others view

adolescence
a period of transition from childhood, often filled with turmoil

Not all teenagers are rebellious and full of conflict – many are cooperative and adjust well to the changes taking place in their lives.

adolescence as a period of great turmoil, stress, rebellion, and negativism (Conger and Peterson, 1984). Adolescence may very well be filled with conflict, storm, and stress, but it is also a period of adjustment that most of us manage to survive quite well. In fact, the picture of the troubled, rebellious, difficult, uncooperative adolescent is probably more of a social stereotype than a reality (Garbarino, 1985; Manning, 1983).

AFTER YOU READ

Task 1 Reading for the main idea

Which of the following is the best single-sentence summary of this text?

1 There are three different ways in which it is possible to define adolescence.
2 The stereotype of the adolescent is that of a rebellious, negative, troubled young person.
3 Adolescence is an exciting period of life.

Task 2 Analyzing paragraph organization

1► Look at the structure of the second paragraph, which is given here in skeleton form, and then answer the questions.

> _____ sentence one _____ . In that case, ____ sentence two ___ .
>
> Or _____ sentence three ___ . This approach ___ sentence four __ .
>
> Additionally, ____ sentence five ____ . Such views __ sentence six _ .
>
> In this context, ___ sentence seven ___ .

1 This paragraph describes three different ways of looking at adolescence. Which sentence or sentences discuss:

   a the first way? _____

   b the second way? _____

   c the third way? _____

2 Which words signal the transition from:

   a the first to the second way? _____

   b the second to the third way? _____

3 Words like *this, that,* and *such* refer back to previous ideas in a paragraph. What previous ideas do the following refer to?

   a In that case, . . .

   b This approach . . .

   c Such views . . .

4 You are often taught in writing classes that a well-written paragraph should have a topic sentence that expresses the main idea of the paragraph. Does this paragraph have a topic sentence? If yes, which one? If no, write a suitable one.

2► Compare answers with a partner.

PREPARING TO READ

Examining graphic material

> **B**efore reading a text, examine any graphs, diagrams, charts, photographs, or illustrations. You can quickly get a good introduction to the content of a text by looking at these visual displays.

Look at Figure 3.1 in the text and answer this question: What are three differences in the way girls and boys grow between the ages of 1 and 19?

1 _____

2 _____

3 _____

Skimming for main ideas

> **R**emember that when you skim, you do not have to read every word. You just need to be able to grasp the organization of a text and its main ideas.

1➤ Skim through the text and write in the number of the paragraph that deals with each of the following topics.

_____ *a* The effects of reaching puberty before most of your peers
_____ *b* The effects of maturing later than most of your peers
_____ *c* The psychological effects of sudden physical changes, such as one's growth spurt
_____ *d* The average ages and rates at which boys and girls increase their height

2➤ Compare answers with a partner.

NOW READ

Now read the text "Physical Change in Adolescence." When you finish, turn to the tasks on page 55.

2   PHYSICAL CHANGE IN ADOLESCENCE

The onset of adolescence is generally marked by two biological or phys- *1* ical changes. First, there is a marked increase in height and weight, known as a **growth spurt**, and second, there is sexual maturation.

The growth spurt of early adolescence usually occurs in girls at an ear- *2* lier age than it does in boys. Girls begin their growth spurt as early as 9 or 10 years of age and then slow down at about age 15. Boys generally show their increased rate of growth between the ages of 12 and 17 years. Indeed, males usually don't reach their adult height until their early 20s, whereas girls generally attain their maximum height by their late teens (Tanner, 1981). Figure 3.1 illustrates one way to represent the adolescent growth spurt in graphic form.

At least some of the potential psychological turmoil of early adoles- *3* cence may be a direct result of the growth spurt. It is not uncommon to find increases in weight and height occurring so rapidly that boys in particular have a hard time coordinating their larger hands and feet and may appear awkward and clumsy. Boys also have the problem of voice change. As their vocal cords grow and lengthen, the pitch of the voice is lowered. Much to the embarrassment of many a teenage boy, this transition is seldom smooth, and the boy may suffer through weeks or months

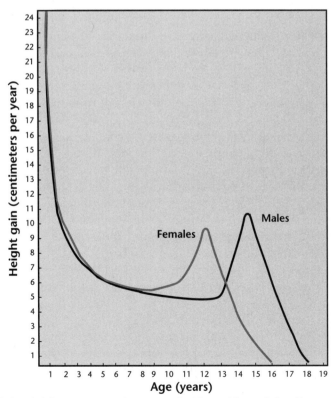

Figure 3.1   Adolescent growth spurts of girls and boys (after Tanner, Whitehouse, and Takaishi, 1966)

Teens develop physically at different rates, with girls typically going through their growth spurt earlier than boys.

of a squeaking, crackling, change of pitch right in the middle of a serious conversation (Adams and Gullota, 1983).

4   Many boys and girls reach puberty before or after most of their peers, or age mates, and are referred to as *early* or *late bloomers*. Reaching puberty well before or well after others of one's age does have some psychological effects, although few are long-lasting. An early blooming girl will probably be taller, stronger, faster, and more athletic than other girls (and many of the boys). She is likely to start dating earlier and to marry at a younger age than her peers. Because of the premium put on physical activity in boys, the early-maturing boy is at a great advantage. He will have more early dating experiences, which will raise his status with his peers.

5   For young teenagers of both sexes, being a late bloomer is more negative in its impact than being an early bloomer (Gross and Duke, 1980). There is some evidence that late-maturing boys carry a sense of inadequacy and poor self-esteem into adulthood. Some late-maturing girls, however, feel – at least in retrospect – that being a late bloomer was an advantage because it offered them an opportunity to develop some broadening interests, rather than becoming "boy-crazy" like so many of their peers in early adolescence (Tobin-Richards et al., 1984). Although generalizations are dangerous, we may suggest that (1) early maturity is more advantageous than later maturity, at least at the time of one's adolescence, and (2) boys profit from early maturity more than girls and may suffer more than girls from later maturity.

6   With all of the physical and physiological changes that occur in early adolescence, it is easy to see why G. Stanley Hall, in the first textbook written about adolescence, was moved to describe the period as one of "second birth" (Hall, 1905).

AFTER YOU READ

Task 1 Reading for detail

According to this text, which is it better to be? Number the following choices in order of best (1) to worst (4).

_____ *a* an early-blooming girl
_____ *b* a late-blooming girl
_____ *c* an early-blooming boy
_____ *d* a late-blooming boy

Task 2 Language focus: Gerunds as subjects

A verb phrase may be the subject of a sentence. Usually when this happens, the *-ing* form of the verb (the gerund) is used.

1➤ Identify the subjects and the verbs in these sentences.

- Reaching puberty well before or well after others of one's age does have some psychological effects. . . . (paragraph 4)
- . . . being a late bloomer is more negative in its impact than being an early bloomer. (paragraph 5)
- Being a late bloomer was an advantage [for some late-maturing girls]. . . . (paragraph 5)

2➤ Complete these sentences with ideas from the text.

1 Being a late bloomer _____ for a boy.
2 Reaching puberty early _____ for a girl.
3 Maturing late _____ for a girl.
4 Being an early bloomer _____ for a boy.

Task 3 Personalizing the topic

> **R**elating new information to your own personal experience is one of the best ways of deepening your understanding of what you have read.

Share the following information about your adolescence with a partner.

1 Did you go through a growth spurt? At what age? Did it cause any problems?
2 Have you stopped growing? At what age did you stop?
3 Were you an early or a late bloomer? If you were either, do you think you had any advantages or disadvantages because of this?

PREPARING TO READ

The SQR3 System (Part I)

> **S**QR3: Survey (S), Question (Q), Read, Recite, and Review (R3)
>
> Many books that teach students how to study at college recommend the SQR3 system for academic reading. The SQR3 system helps you become an active reader. Active readers do not simply pick up a text and read it. They perform a series of tasks before reading, while reading, and after reading; tasks that help them understand and remember what they have read.

In this prereading activity we will look at the first three steps in the SQR3 system only: survey, question, and read.

1➤ *Survey* When you survey a text before reading it closely, you look at titles, headings, subheadings, graphs, charts, pictures, terms in bold or italics, and skim through the text, reading the beginnings and ends of some paragraphs. Look at this text and survey it. Report back to the class on what you looked at and discovered.

2➤ *Question* Before they read a text, active readers formulate questions that they think the text will answer. As they read, they keep checking to see if their questions are being answered.

As a result of your survey of the text, "Cognitive and Social Development in Adolescence," you can begin to formulate questions. How do you do this? One trick is to look at the headings, subheadings, and key terms that you noticed in your survey and turn them into questions. For example, the title of this text may suggest the following questions:

- What cognitive changes occur in adolescence?
- How does an adolescent develop socially? What changes take place?

Now survey this text again. Write questions in the margins that you expect to have answered as you read the text. When you go through steps R3 – read, recite, and review – you will keep returning to these questions, asking yourself if you are able to answer them.

3➤ *Read* Imagine your instructor gave you an open-book test. As you were taking the test, you would look at the text to find the answers to the instructor's questions. When you read using the SQR3 system, you should read in the same way, always thinking about the questions that you want to have answered.

NOW READ

Now read the text "Cognitive and Social Development in Adolescence," with your questions in mind. When you finish the text, turn to the tasks that begin on page 61.

3 COGNITIVE AND SOCIAL DEVELOPMENT IN ADOLESCENCE

Adolescence is a developmental period in which, according to Piaget, one is now able to think abstractly and to imagine, to think about what is and to ponder what might be. This new, higher level of mental operations often gets turned toward self-analysis, toward a contemplation of one's self in a social context (Keating, 1980). In this section, we'll examine three issues related to cognitive and social processes in adolescent development: identity formation, adolescent egocentrism, and the influence of family.

IDENTITY FORMATION

Adolescents give the impression of being great experimenters. They experiment with hair styles, music, religions, drugs, sexual outlets, fad diets, part-time jobs, part-time relationships, and part-time philosophies of life. In fact, it often seems that teenagers' commitments are made on a part-time basis. They are busily trying things out, doing things their way, off on a grand search for Truth.

This perception of adolescents as experimenters is not without foundation. It is consistent with the view that one of the major tasks of adolescence is the resolution of an *identity crisis* – the struggle to define and integrate the sense of who one is, what one is to do in life, and what one's attitudes, beliefs, and values should be. During adolescence, we come to grips with many questions: "Who am I?" "What am I going to do with my life?" "What is the point of it all?" Needless to say, these are not trivial questions. A person's search for his or her identity may lead to conflicts. Some of these conflicts may be resolved very easily, some continue into adulthood.

Adolescence is a time for experimentation and searching for one's identity.

The concept of *identity formation* is associated with the personality theorist Erik Erikson. For Erikson, the search for identity is the fifth of eight stages of psychosocial development. It is the stage that occurs during the adolescent years. For some youngsters, adolescence brings very little confusion or conflict at all in terms of attitudes, beliefs, or values. Many teenagers are quite able and willing to accept without question the values and sense of self that they began to develop in childhood.

For many teenagers, however, the conflict of identity is quite real. They have a sense of giving up the values of parents and teachers in favor of new ones – their own. On the other hand, physical growth, physiological changes, increased sexuality, and perceived societal pressures to decide what they want to be when they "grow up" may lead to what Erikson calls *role confusion.* Wanting to be independent, to be one's self, often does not fit in with the values of the past, of childhood. Hence, the teenager tries to experiment with different possibilities in an attempt to see what works out best, occasionally to the dissatisfaction of bewildered parents.

ADOLESCENT EGOCENTRISM

Egocentrism – a focusing on one's self and an inability to take the point of view of others – was used by Piaget to describe part of the cognitive functioning of young children (between the ages of 2 and 6). David Elkind (1981, 1984) uses the term egocentrism in a slightly different way. In **adolescent egocentrism**, not only do individuals engage in self-centered thinking, but they also come to believe that virtually everyone else is thinking about them, too. Because they can now think abstractly, adolescents begin to think about the thoughts of others and have a tendency to believe that they are usually the focus of attention. Needless to say, adolescent egocentrism often leads to a heightened sense of self-consciousness.

adolescent egocentrism
the belief of many adolescents – usually erroneous – that they are the focus of everyone else's attention

Many young teens are painfully self-conscious and may develop false beliefs that people are talking about them and judging them.

Elkind proposes two particular manifestations of adolescent egocentrism. For one thing, teenagers often feel that they are constantly "on stage," performing. They become quite convinced that when they enter a room, everyone is watching them and making judgments about everything – from what they are wearing to how their hair is styled. Now, in truth, it may be that no one is watching, but the youngster believes that they are. Elkind calls this the construction of an *imaginary audience*. Coming to think that everyone is watching and analyzing you is explanation enough for the extreme self-consciousness of many young teens, argues Elkind (Elkind and Bowen, 1979).

Adolescents often tend to overemphasize their own importance. They are, after all, the focus of their own attention, and given their imaginary audience, they feel the are the focus of everyone else's attention as well. As a result, they tend to develop some rather unrealistic cognitions about themselves, which Elkind calls *personal fables*. These are essentially stories about themselves that teenagers generate, often on the basis of irrational beliefs. They come to believe (egocentrically) that no harm can come to them. They won't become addicted after trying a drug at a party. Their driving won't be affected by alcohol consumption. They won't get pregnant. Those sorts of things happen to others. These sorts of beliefs (cognitions) can be dangerous, of course, and they can be the source of considerable parental aggravation.

THE INFLUENCE OF FAMILY

No matter what label we give it, one of the major processes involved in adolescence is separating in some real way from one's family. With the emergence of one's own identity comes independence and autonomy. The resulting conflict for teenagers is often very real. On the one hand, they want to become autonomous and strike out on their own. At the

Most teenagers report that they prefer a democratic parenting style in which parents give advice, set limits, but allow for independence.

same time, they sense a sadness and even fear over giving up the security of home and family.

How adolescents resolve conflicts they have with their parents often hinges significantly on what is termed parental style. Psychologists have identified three major approaches used by parents in dealing with their adolescent children. (It should be pointed out quickly that few parents adopt and use one and only one style). The *authoritarian* style of parenting decrees that, "You should do so, because I say so!" As often as not, the adolescent isn't even allowed to express his or her beliefs. The teenager is seen as a member of low standing in family affairs. Not surprisingly, this style of parenting behavior often leads to rebellion, alienation, and more conflict. On the other hand, the authoritarian style can lead to submissiveness and conformity, which, for the emerging teenager, is maladaptive. The style of parenting called *permissive* is in many ways at the other extreme from the authoritarian style. Here, the teenager has an almost free rein. Parents are supportive, but set few limits. The style most recommended is usually called *democratic*. Here, parents act as experts, give advice, and do set limits, but they also consult with the teenager, allow some independence of choice, and involve the teenager in decision making.

Most teenagers feel that their parents use a democratic style, and they value that style (Kelly and Godwin, 1983). Reports of family difficulties with adolescents can often be traced to either an overly authoritarian or overly permissive style (Baumrind, 1978; Collins, 1982).

AFTER YOU READ

Task 1 Note-taking in the margins

Taking notes while you read can be an effective study tool. Some students like to write notes in the margins of their textbooks. These are called marginal notes. Others prefer to use a separate notebook.

1➤ Work with a partner and discuss the following questions.

1 What are the advantages of marginal notes over notes in a notebook?
2 What are the disadvantages of marginal notes over notes in a notebook?
3 Which do you prefer? Why?

2➤ Look at the sample marginal notes taken on a portion of this text, shown in Figure A on page 62. Answer these questions with a partner.

1 What abbreviations does the note-taker use?
2 What kind of information does the note-taker put in the margins of the text?
3 How does the note-taker identify key terms, their definitions, and important names?
4 How does the note-taker draw attention to examples or details in the text?

3➤ Look at the portion of the text under the heading, "Adolescent Egocentrism" on page 58 and make marginal notes as directed in the following list of steps.

1 Highlight the following key terms and their definitions.

- egocentrism
- adolescent egocentrism
- imaginary audience
- personal fables

2 Draw vertical lines and put the following notes next to them, opposite the parts of the text to which they refer.

What is Adol. Egocent?
Piaget def. of Egocent (2 – 6 yr olds)
Elkind def. of Adol. Egocent
Ex. of adol. self-consciousness
Exs. of dangerous unrealistic beliefs

3 Underline and put an asterisk next to the phrase "two particular manifestations of adolescent egocentrism," and then draw two lines from the word "two": one line to the term *imaginary audience* and the other to *personal fables*.

4 Write the numbers *1, 2,* and *3* in the text over the three examples of dangerous beliefs teenagers have.

4➤ Make your own marginal notes for the third section of this reading, "The Influence of Family." Compare your marginal notes with a partner's notes.

IDENTITY FORMATION

What is identity formation?

Adolescents give the impression of being great experimenters. They experiment with hair styles, music, religions, drugs, sexual outlets, fad diets, part-time jobs, part-time relationships, and part-time philosophies of life. In fact, it often seems that teenagers' commitments are made on a part-time basis. They are busily trying things out, doing things their way, off on a grand search for Truth.

Things adols. like to experiment w/

This perception of adolescents as experimenters is not without foundation. It is consistent with the view that one of the major tasks of adolescence is the resolution of an *identity crisis* – the struggle to define and integrate the sense of who one is, what one is to do in life, and what one's attitudes, beliefs, and values should be. During adolescence, we come to grips with many questions: "Who am I?" "What am I going to do with my life?" "What is the point of it all?" Needless to say, these are not trivial questions. A person's search for his or her identity may lead to conflicts. Some of these conflicts may be resolved very easily, some continue into adulthood.

Def. of identity crisis

The big questions adols. ask

The concept of *identity formation* is associated with the personality theorist Erik Erikson. For Erikson, the search for identity is the fifth of eight stages of psychosocial development. It is the stage that occurs during the adolescent years. For some youngsters, adolescence brings very little confusion or conflict at all in terms of attitudes, beliefs, or values. Many teenagers are quite able and willing to accept without question the values and sense of self that they began to develop in childhood.

Not all adols. question values

For many teenagers, however, the conflict of identity is quite real. They have a sense of giving up the values of parents and teachers in favor of new ones – their own. On the other hand, physical growth, physiological changes, and increased sexuality, and perceived societal pressures to decide what they want to be when they "grow up" may lead to what Erikson calls *role confusion*. Wanting to be independent, to be one's self, often does not fit in with the values of the past, of childhood. Hence, the teenager tries to experiment with different possibilities in an attempt to see what works out best, occasionally to the dissatisfaction of bewildered parents.

Conflict = own values vs parents

Causes of role confusion

Figure A   Sample marginal notes on "Cognitive and Social Development in Adolescence"

Task 2 The SQR3 System (Part II)

> The SQR3 system includes not only prereading strategies, but also strategies to use after reading a text.

1➤ *Recite*   The fourth step in the SQR3 system is to recite. To recite is to say aloud from memory. After you read a section of text you should stop and ask yourself, "Now what did I just read? Do I understand the main ideas? Can I answer the questions that I thought this text would answer for me?"

Choose one of the three parts of the text, "Cognitive and Social Development in Adolescence." Reread it. Then give an oral summary to a student who read a different part of the text.

2➤ *Review*   When you review a section or chapter of a textbook, you should go back and skim the text, placing a check (√) next to the parts of the text that you are sure you understand and a question mark (?) next to those parts that are still unclear to you and that you need to study further.

Review the whole text, "Cognitive and Social Development in Adolescence," placing checks and question marks where appropriate.

Task 3 Personalizing the topic

Answer to the following questions with your classmates. Explain each answer fully.

1 During your adolescence were you a "great experimenter"?
2 During your adolescence did you go through an identity crisis?
3 Can you relate to the concepts of an imaginary audience and personal fables? Did you feel any of these things when you were an adolescent?
4 What style of parenting did your parents adopt? Do you approve of this style? What style of parenting do you believe is best?

Task 4 Writing a summary

> Reciting and reviewing, as in the SQR3 system, is only one way to ensure that you have understood a text. Writing a short summary is another good way to help you digest new information in a text and fix it in your memory.

Choose one of the three parts of this text and write a short summary.

PREPARING TO READ

Predicting the content

In this text you will read about the leading causes of death among teenagers in the United States. Which of the following do you think ranks as the number 1 leading cause of death, the number 2 cause, and so on? In the box, list the following causes in your predicted rank order.

murder   *suicide*   *accidents*   *disease*

Rank	Cause of death
1	_____
2	_____
3	_____
4	_____

Skimming for main ideas

Skim through the text, and decide which paragraph deals with each of the following topics. Write the number of the paragraph in the blank.

_____ *a* factors leading to teenage suicide
_____ *b* things that need to be done to reduce the suicide rate
_____ *c* statistics about teenage suicide

NOW READ

Now read the text "Teenage Suicide." When you finish, check the rank order you predicted for causes of death among teenagers. Then turn to the tasks that begin on page 67.

4   TEENAGE SUICIDE

The death of any young person is a tragic and sad occurrence. When that 1
death is the result of suicide, our emotional reaction is often magnified.
As a final solution to perceived problems, suicide is certainly final, but it
solves little. Rates of successful and failed suicide attempts among the
young are definitely on the increase (for example, Curran, 1987).
Holinger (1978) estimates a 131 percent increase in successful suicide
attempts between 1961 and 1975. Colt (1983) claims a 300 percent
increase since 1960. Peck (1982) suggests that more than one million adolescents think seriously about killing themselves each year. After accidents and murder, suicide is the third leading killer of teenagers.

*The news that a teenage friend has committed suicide sometimes leads others to con-
sider taking their own lives.*

In an effort to determine why so many young people turn to suicide, 2
Allen (1987) recently surveyed the research literature and came up with
a number of helpful insights. Allen suggests that there are many general
determinants of suicide. These are broad, *predisposing factors*. In addition,
there are a number of *predictors* of suicide, which usually are found
through some sort of psychological testing or assessment. And finally,
there are *precipitating events* that may lead directly to an attempt at suicide. These determinants, predictors, and precipitating events are summarized in Figure 3.2.

What can be done to begin to stem the tide of teenage suicide? Allen 3
suggests a number of things can be done, and most revolve around education. First, we all must realize that suicide among teenagers is a real
and present problem, and we must bring discussions of suicide out into

Predisposing factors (general background variables)

1. **Family.** Family problems such as divorce, poor communication, strict parental control, and alcoholism; alcohol use in the family may be more important than alcohol use by the youngster
2. **Peers.** Isolation from peers or having no good relations with people your own age
3. **A difficult birth.** (Surprisingly) difficulty at or soon after birth may predispose for later problems
4. **Personal factors.** Low self-esteem; drug/alcohol use; loss of boy/girlfriend; poor academic performance; loss of a close friend; depression (the highest single predictor); sex (most suicide attempts are by females, most successes by males)
5. **Technological advance.** The inability to handle new technology may lead some to a sense of helplessness, perhaps despair
6. **Acceptance of suicide.** Knowing other people or about other people who have committed suicide may lead to the feeling that suicide is acceptable
7. **Mobility and rootlessness.** Moving frequently may lead to a lack of long-term relationships that could be used for support

Predictors (diagnoses from psychological tests)

1. **Depression.** Many measures of depression are related to suicide
2. **Control.** Believing that one's life is under the control of others including fate and chance
3. **Hopelessness.** May be more important than depression, perhaps even the cause of depression

Precipitating events (factors that lead directly to suicide attempts)

1. **Clustering.** Sometimes teen suicides come in "clusters," that is, several at a time in a community; it becomes "contagious" – the thing to do, like a fashion!
2. **Independent traumatic events.** Things beyond the control of the individual, such as death or loss of a close friend or relative, parental divorce, sudden money problems
3. **Nonindependent events.** Events caused by the suicidal individual, such as drug or alcohol consumption, purchase of a gun, pregnancy when not married, accidents resulting from deliberately dangerous behaviors

Figure 3.2 Some of the general determinants of suicide among adolescents (list modified from Allen, 1987)

the open. In addition, we must all learn the signs and symptoms of impending suicide. Peers must be educated to be good and open listeners and to suggest therapy and professional help for friends and acquaintances who may be contemplating suicide. When one considers the cost in terms of grief, as well as in terms of lost human resources, there is ample reason for our commitment to efforts to mount a national campaign against suicide.

AFTER YOU READ

Task 1 Reading for detail

Answer the following questions. Then compare answers with a partner.

1 Which one of the following statements is true according to this text? (Check one.)

__ a Failed suicide attempts have gone up, but successful suicide attempts have gone down in recent years.

__ b Both failed and successful suicide attempts have gone up.

__ c Successful suicide attempts have gone up, but failed attempts have gone down.

__ d There has been little change in the suicide rate over the last few years.

2 How did Allen come up with his three different categories of determinants for suicide? (Check all that apply.)

__ a He interviewed young people.

__ b He visited and observed families who had teenagers who had attempted suicide.

__ c He read studies of teenage suicide cases.

__ d He read novels in which teenagers committed suicide.

3 Five suggestions are given in the final paragraph concerning what can be done to "stem the tide" of teenage suicide. List all five.

1 _____

2 _____

3 _____

4 _____

5 _____

Task 2 Applying what you read: Analyzing new data

> Finding ways to apply new knowledge is a great way to deepen your understanding of new subject matter. This is why your professor may well give you a case-study activity like the following, in which you are asked to apply what you have learned to analyze new data.

1➤ Read the following profiles of four different teenagers. As you read, refer to Figure

3.2 in the text to help you find which of the determining factors each teenager has. Then identify the teenagers with the highest and lowest suicide risks.

Case Study 1: Greta Pearson

Greta Pearson is 16 years old. She has just discovered that she is pregnant. She lives alone with her mother, who does not work and spends most of her time drunk in front of the television. Her father left home when she was 4, which was the last time she saw him. Her mother never remarried and she has no brothers and sisters, but she does have several close girlfriends. Greta is an intelligent girl who does well at school. Her boyfriend is also 16. Two weeks ago their relationship came to an end when he found another girl-friend.

Case Study 2: Roger Lopez

Roger Lopez is 17. He was kicked out of school last year because he was found selling and using drugs. While he was at school, he was tested by psychologists who found he measured very high on a scale measuring a sense of hopelessness. He lives with his parents. He has a good relationship with his mother, but his father is very strict with him. Roger's father will not let him play his music in the house or have his friends at the house, for example. A few weeks ago, Roger bought a gun.

Case Study 3: Henry Matthieson

Henry Matthieson is 17, too. He lives in a small farming community, where everyone knows everyone else and where there is only one high school. He lives in the house that he was born in. Recently two of the kids in his class killed themselves. Nobody knows why. Now he is feeling depressed and wonders if life is worth living. He has never been good academically at school, nor is he good at sports. He has never had a girlfriend. He comes from a large family. His parents are religious; they do not drink and are very strict.

Case Study 4: Lucy Wong

Until a few weeks ago, Lucy Wong (18) thought she came from a wealthy family. Then her father came home and told the family that he had lost all his money in a bad investment. Now her mother wants to divorce her father. Lucy's family has moved many times in the last twelve years. In fact, she has been to ten different schools since first grade. She often finds herself feeling depressed and recently she has started to steal alcohol from her parents' cupboard. Last year her parents bought her a new car, but a week ago she went driving after she had been drinking and totaled it. Luckily she was not hurt.

2➤ Form a group with classmates who have identified a different student as being the highest suicide risk. Explain why you think your choice is more likely to be correct.

CHAPTER 3 Writing assignment

Choose one of the following topics as your chapter writing assignment.

1 Analyze your own adolescence using the concepts that are found in this chapter, for example, identity crisis, adolescent egocentrism, and so on.

2 In this chapter we read about the "bewildered" parents of adolescents. Are there many bewildered parents in your country? What is the best role for parents to adopt while their children are going through adolescence?

3 Is teenage suicide a problem in your country? If yes, what do you think are its main causes, and what is done to help prevent teenage suicide? If no, what is it about your culture that helps to discourage teenage suicide?

PREPARING TO READ

Personalizing the topic

According to this text, young adults have to face many difficult questions. Which of these questions, taken from the text, have you ever seriously asked yourself? Put a check (√) in front of those that apply.

_____ *1* Should I get married?

_____ *2* Should I live with someone?

_____ *3* Should I get a job?

_____ *4* To what sort of career should I devote my life?

_____ *5* Do I need more education?

_____ *6* Where should I go to get more education?

_____ *7* Should I have children?

_____ *8* When should I have children?

Building vocabulary: Collocations

> **W**hen learning vocabulary in English, it is always a good idea to be aware of *collocations*, or combinations of words that often occur together. (For example, some verbs are often followed by – or collocate with – certain nouns.)The more you are aware of collocations, the easier reading becomes.

1► Each of the verbs and nouns in the following lists occurs in this text. Choose the verb that you think collocates with each noun and write it in the blank. If you think more than one verb is possible, write them both down.

Verbs		*Nouns*
to take	*1* _____	a career
to attain	*2* _____	advice
to make	*3* _____	adult status
to seek	*4* _____	a decision
to pursue	*5* _____	responsibility
to address	*6* _____	money
to follow	*7* _____	a family
to raise	*8* _____	a path
to earn	*9* _____	a choice
	10 _____	an issue

2► Compare answers with a partner.

NOW READ

Now read the text "Early Adulthood." When you finish, turn to the tasks on page 73.

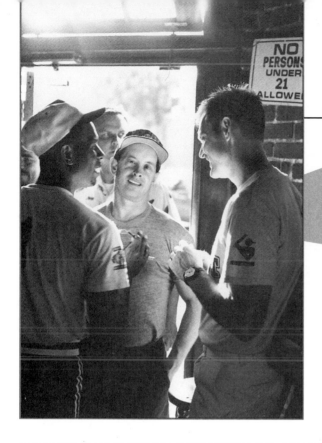

Adulthood

1 EARLY ADULTHOOD

Our adult lives end with our deaths. Just when **adulthood** begins is difficult to say. In a legal sense, adult status is often granted by governments – at age 18 for some activities, or at age 21 for others. Psychologically speaking, adulthood is marked by two possibilities that at first seem contradictory: (1) independence, in the sense of taking responsibility for one's actions and no longer being tied to parents; (2) interdependence, in the sense of building new commitments and intimacies in interpersonal relationships.

With the attainment of adult status, there are new and often difficult choices to be made. Advice may be sought from elders, parents, teachers, or friends, but as adults, individuals make their own choices. Should I get married? Should I stay single? Perhaps I should live with someone. Should I get a job? Which one? To what sort of career should I devote my life? Do I need more education? What sort of education? Where? How? Should we have children? How many? When? Now, while we're young, or should we wait until we're more experienced and have our careers established? Many of these issues are first addressed in adolescence, during identity formation. But, for the adult, these questions are no longer abstract. They are very real questions that demand some sort of response.

One of the most pressing decisions at this time of one's life is what career to pursue. However, with so many possibilities to choose from, this decision is often a difficult one to make. In addition, there are many factors that may influence an individual in the choice of a career and

adulthood
the period of life after childhood and adolescence; there is no specific age at which it begins, except for some limited legal purposes

This young couple will need all their youthful energy to cope with the challenges of early adulthood.

some of these may be conflicting. For example, family pressure, the potential for earning money, and one's own personal interest may all be factors that pull an individual in three different directions when trying to decide what career path to follow. Although it is often assumed that by the time a person is a young adult they will know what they want to "do with their life," in fact the process of finding a career may take a long time. It is not uncommon for an individual to try more than one career before finding the one that leads to job satisfaction.

Clearly young adulthood is a period of stress. It is a time for raising a family, finding and maintaining the "right" job, and keeping a balance among self, family, job, and society at large. It is a period of life that requires great energy. Fortunately, in terms of physical development, we are at something of a peak during our 20s and 30s. As Levinson (1986) has stated, "early adulthood is the era of greatest energy and abundance and of greatest contradiction and stress."

AFTER YOU READ

Task 1 Reading for detail

Answer the following questions with a partner.

1 According to this text, adult status can be granted for some activities at one age and for other activities at another age. Give examples to illustrate this.

2 "Psychologically speaking, adulthood is marked by two possibilities that at first seem contradictory." Explain.

3 According to the second paragraph, in what areas of life does a young adult have to make some difficult decisions?

4 Why does the writer state that the factors that may influence an individual in the choice of a career may be "conflicting"?

5 Why does the writer use the word "fortunately" in the fourth paragraph?

Task 2 Personalizing the topic

1➤ Read the statements that follow and put a check (√) in front of those that have influenced why you have chosen or might choose a particular career for yourself.

_____ 1 I want to make as much money as possible.

_____ 2 I want to help my family.

_____ 3 I want to pursue my personal interests and hobbies.

_____ 4 I want to have lots of exciting experiences.

_____ 5 I want to make a contribution to society/humankind.

_____ 6 I want a career that gives me as much free time as possible.

2➤ Explain your choices to a partner.

Task 3 Personal writing

> **M**any language learners keep a private journal and write about personal events and ideas. It is a good way to practice writing in a second language without worrying too much about accuracy or a teacher's grade. When you read about a topic that interests you, even in an academic textbook, why not take some time to write down your personal thoughts on the topic?

Write briefly about the factors that have influenced (or will influence) your choice of career.

PREPARING TO READ

How much do you already know?

> **B**y mentally surveying what you already know about a topic before you start reading, you will be more likely to read actively and critically. As you read, you will be checking to see if the information in the text agrees with or disagrees with your knowledge.

How much do you know about Americans and marriage? The answers to the following questions are given in this text on early adulthood. Before you read, choose what you think are the correct answers.

1 Compared to 30 years ago, what change has there been in the average age at which Americans get married?
  a They are getting married younger.
  b They are getting married older.
  c There has been no significant change.

2 What percentage of Americans gets married at least once?
  a 65 percent   *b* 80 percent   *c* 95 percent

3 What would most Americans rate as the single most important factor leading to happiness in adult life?
  a a successful marriage   *b* an active community life   *c* many close friendships

4 Most Americans are likely to marry someone who _____.
  a is similar to them in most ways.
  b is different from them in most ways.
  c is similar to them in some ways and different in others.

5 Americans are most likely to marry someone similar to them in _____.
  a race   *b* age   *c* educational background

6 Research has been done to find out which qualities American men and women find most desirable in a spouse. Which one of these statements do you expect to be true?
  a Men rank intelligence over attractiveness; women do the opposite.
  b Women rank intelligence over attractiveness; men do the opposite.
  c Both men and women rank intelligence over attractiveness.

7 Approximately what percentage of first marriages in the United States end in divorce?
  a 40 percent *b* 55 percent   *c* 70 percent

8 Approximately how many years does the average American marriage last?
  a 4   *b* 9   *c* 14

NOW READ

Now read the text "Marriage and Family." When you have finished, check to see whether you answered the questions correctly, then turn to the tasks that begin on page 78.

2   MARRIAGE AND FAMILY

It is Erikson's claim that early adulthood revolves around the basic choice of intimacy versus isolation. A failure to establish close, loving, or intimate relationships is said to result in loneliness and long periods of social isolation. Marriage is certainly not the only source of interpersonal intimacy, but it is still the first choice for most Americans. More young adults than ever before are postponing marriage plans, but fully 95 percent of us do marry (at least once). In fact, we are more likely to claim that happiness in adult life depends more on a successful marriage than any other factor, including friendship, community activities, or hobbies (Glenn and Weaver, 1981).

Most Americans get married at least once.

Individuals reach the point of being ready to marry at different ages. Some may decide to marry simply because they perceive that it is the thing to do. Others choose marriage as an expression of an intimacy that has already developed (Stinnett, 1984). In addition to the choices of when (and how) to marry, of no small consequence is the choice of whom to marry. If we have learned nothing else about the choice of marriage partners over the last thirty years, it is that mate selection is a complex process.

MATE SELECTION

Psychologist David Buss has reviewed the available evidence on mate selection with a particular focus on the question of whether or not opposites attract. He concluded that at least in marriage, they do not. He found that "we are likely to marry someone who is similar to us in almost every variable" (Buss, 1985). Most important are matters of age, education, race, religion, and ethnic background (in order), followed by attitudes and opinions, mental abilities, socioeconomic status, height,

Rank	Male choices	Female choices
1	kindness and understanding	kindness and understanding
2	intelligence	intelligence
3	physical attractiveness	exciting personality
4	exciting personality	good health
5	good health	adaptability
6	adaptability	physical attractiveness
7	creativity	creativity
8	desire for children	good earning capacity
9	college graduate	college graduate
10	good heredity	desire for children
11	good earning capacity	good heredity
12	good housekeeper	good housekeeper
13	religious orientation	religious orientation

Figure 4.1 Characteristics sought in mates (from Buss and Barnes, 1986)

weight, and even eye color. More than that, he found that men and women are in nearly complete agreement on those characteristics they commonly seek in a mate (Buss, 1985; Buss and Barnes, 1986). Figure 4.1 presents 13 such characteristics ranked by men and women. There is a significant difference in ranking for only two: good earning potential and physical attractiveness.

You should not conclude from this discussion that choosing a marriage partner is always a matter of making a sound, rational decision. Clearly it isn't. The truth is that many factors, including romantic love, affect such decisions. The fact that approximately 40 percent of all first marriages end in divorce and that, in the United States, 9.4 years is the average life span of a marriage are unsettling reminders that the choices people make are not always the best. Just as men and women agree on what matters in choosing a mate, so do they agree on what matters in maintaining a marriage, listing first such matters as liking one's spouse as a friend, agreeing on goals, and a mutual concern for making the marriage work (Lauer and Lauer, 1985).

PARENTHOOD

Beyond establishing an intimate relationship, becoming a parent is generally taken as a sure sign of adulthood. For many young couples, parenthood has become more a matter of choice than ever before because of more available means of contraception and new treatments for infertility. Having one's own family helps foster the process of *generativity* that Erikson associates with middle adulthood. This process reflects a growing concern for family and for one's impact on future generations

The awareness that one can have an impact on future generations is an important developmental stage of life – obviously this occurs most powerfully with parenthood.

Parenting adds one more challenging role for the adult who may still be struggling with the role of working adult and spouse.

(Chilman, 1980). Although such concerns may not become central until one is over 40, parenthood usually begins much sooner.

There is no doubt that having a baby around the house significantly changes established routines, often leading to negative consequences (Miller and Sollie, 1980). The freedom for spontaneous trips, intimate outings, and privacy is in large measure given up in trade for the joys of parenthood. As parents, men and women take on new responsibilities of new social roles – that of father and mother. These new roles of adulthood add to the already established roles of being a male or a female, a son or a daughter, a husband or a wife, and so on. There seems to be little doubt that choosing to have children (or at least choosing to have a large number of children) is becoming less and less popular (Schaie and Willis, 1986). Although many people still regard the decision not to have children as basically selfish, irresponsible, and immoral, there is little evidence that such a decision leads to a decline in well-being or satisfaction later in life (Beckman and Houser, 1982; Keith, 1983).

AFTER YOU READ

Task 1 Language focus: Expressing confidence in the truth or accuracy of a fact

1➤ Read these two sentences taken from the final paragraph of the text. Notice how in each one a fact is qualified by an introductory clause that shows the degree of confidence or doubt that the writer has in the truth or accuracy of the fact.

> There is no doubt that having a baby around the house changes established routines, often leading to negative consequences.

> There is little evidence that such a decision [not to have children] leads to a decline in well-being or satisfaction later in life.

2➤ The following chart shows more ways in which a fact may be qualified in order to express different degrees of confidence in its truth or accuracy. Choose expressions from this chart to qualify statements 1–6 below. Base your answers on information that you find in the text. The first one has been done for you.

There is There seems to be	a great deal of some little no	doubt evidence (to suggest)	that . . .

1 Fewer Americans are choosing to ever get married.

There seems to be little evidence to suggest that fewer Americans are choosing to ever get married.

2 Most Americans believe that having a successful marriage leads to a happy life.

3 Americans tend to marry someone who is opposite to themselves in many ways.

4 It is difficult to have a successful marriage.

5 On the whole, men and women value very different qualities in a mate.

6 Women are more concerned than men about whether their spouse has good earning capacity.

3➤ Compare answers with a partner and explain why you chose to express the amount of doubt or evidence in the way that you did.

Task 2 Personalizing the topic

Discuss the following questions in groups.

1 Is it important to get married? Is there a best age at which to get married?

2 Is it important to have children? Is there a best age to start having children? What is the best number of children to have?

3 Which is it most important for you to have in common with your mate:
   - the same age?
   - the same education?
   - the same religion?
   - the same attitudes and opinions?
   - the same socioeconomic status?

4 Which qualities do you most wish for in a mate? Look at Figure 4.1 on page 75 and choose the three most important and the three least important qualities.

Most important	Least important
1 _____	1 _____
2 _____	2 _____
3 _____	3 _____

Task 3 Personal writing

Write briefly on one of these topics.

1 Why I Never Want to Get Married

2 Why I Want to Get Married

3 Why I Got Married

PREPARING TO READ

Thinking about the topic

At about the age of 40, a number of physical changes begin to take place in people. Make a list of five to eight such items. Here are some sentence starters to give you ideas:

The hair begins to . . .

The muscles begin to . . .

The stomach begins to . . .

The skin begins to . . .

Compare lists with your classmates.

Building vocabulary: Guessing meaning from context

> You do not need to look up every word that you do not know in the dictionary. It is often possible to get a general idea of the meaning of a word or phrase from its context.

Read the following passage from the text and use the context to work out what the words in bold probably mean.

> The movement to middle adulthood involves a **transition** filled with reexamination – at least for men (Levinson, 1986). During the middle years, one is forced to **contemplate** one's own **mortality**. The so-called **middle-age spread**, loss of muscle tone, **facial wrinkles**, and **graying** hair are evident each day in the mirror. At about the age of 40, **sensory capacities** and abilities begin slowly to diminish. Most people in this stage now notice **obituaries** in the newspaper, where more and more people of the same age or even younger are listed every day.

transition _____

contemplate _____

mortality _____

middle-age spread _____

facial wrinkles _____

graying _____

sensory capacities _____

obituaries _____

NOW READ

Now read the text "Middle Adulthood." When you finish, turn to the tasks on page 83.

3   MIDDLE ADULTHOOD

As the middle years of adulthood approach, many aspects of life become *1*
settled. By the time most people reach the age of 40, their place in the
framework of society is fairly well set. They have chosen their life-style
and have grown accustomed to it. They have a family (or have decided
not to). They have chosen what is to be their major life work or career.
"Most of us during our 40s and 50s become 'senior members' in our own
particular worlds, however grand or modest they may be" (Levinson,
1986).

   The movement to middle adulthood involves transition filled with *2*
reexamination – at least for men (Levinson et al., 1974). During the middle years, one is forced to contemplate one's own mortality. The so-called
middle-age spread, loss of muscle tone, facial wrinkles, and graying hair
are evident each day in the mirror. At about the age of 40, sensory capacities and abilities begin slowly to diminish. Most people in this stage now
notice obituaries in the newspaper, where more and more people of the
same age or even younger are listed every day.

   For some people, perhaps for men more than women, the realization *3*
that time is running out produces something of a crisis, even approach-
ing panic. For most, however, middle age is a time of great satisfaction
and true opportunity (Rossi, 1980). In most cases, children are grown.
Careers are in full bloom. Time is available as never before for leisure and
commitment to community, perhaps in the form of volunteer work.

*By middle adulthood most people have chosen careers and life-styles and have more
time for leisure activities.*

This can be a difficult time for some, usually women, who have to care for their parents and their children at the same time.

4   Robert Havighurst (1972) says there are seven major tasks that one must face in the middle years:

1   *Accepting and adjusting to the physiological changes of middle age* Although there certainly are many physical activities that middle-age persons can engage in, they sometimes must be selective or must modify the vigor with which they attack such activities.

2   *Reaching and maintaining satisfactory performance in one's occupation* If career satisfaction is not attained, one may attempt a mid-career job change. And, of course, changing jobs in middle age is often more a matter of necessity than choice. In either case, the potential for further growth and development or for crisis and conflict exists.

3   *Adjusting to aging parents* This can be a major concern, particularly for women in the middle (Brody, 1981) who are caring for their own children and parents at the same time. In spite of widespread opinions to the contrary, individual concern and responsibility for the care of the elderly has not deteriorated in recent years (Brody, 1985).

4   *Assisting teenage children to become happy and responsible adults* During the middle years of adulthood, parents see their children mature into and through adolescence. Helping to prepare them for adulthood and independence (leaving the nest) becomes a task viewed with ambivalence.

5   *Achieving adult social and civic responsibility* This task is very much like what Erikson calls the crisis of generativity versus stagnation. People often shift from thinking about all that they have done with their life to considering what they will do with what time is left for them and how they can leave a mark on future generations (Erikson, 1963; Harris, 1983).

6   *Relating to one's spouse as a person*, and

7   *Developing leisure-time activities* Although all seven of these tasks are clearly related and interdependent, this is particularly true of the last two. As children leave home and financial concerns diminish, there is more time for one's spouse and for leisure. Taking advantage of these changes in meaningful ways provides a unique challenge for some adults whose whole lives have been previously devoted to children and career.

AFTER YOU READ

Task 1 Reading for main ideas

Each of the following four statements summarizes one of the four paragraphs in this text. (The last paragraph contains a list of seven items.) Number the statements according to the paragraphs they summarize.

___ *a* By middle adulthood, one's family and career have usually been established.

___ *b* During this period, some people go through a mid-life crisis, while others achieve great personal satisfaction.

___ *c* There are a number of challenges in middle adulthood.

___ *d* One becomes more and more aware of physical changes as one grows older.

Task 2 Applying what you read

1➤ According to Havighurst, there are seven major challenges or tasks that people usually have to face during middle adulthood. They are listed in the box.

Consider a middle-aged person whom you know well (perhaps one of your parents). Put a check (√) next to the challenges that this person has faced as an adult.

The Challenges of Middle Adulthood

My _____ has had to face these challenges:

(name of your relationship to this person, for example aunt, friend)

1 adjusting to physiological changes of middle age ❑

2 reaching a point in his or her career with which he or she is satisfied ❑

3 taking care of aging parents ❑

4 trying to help teenage children become responsible adults ❑

5 finding ways to play a role in the community ❑

6 developing a stronger relationship with his or her spouse ❑

7 finding new hobbies or leisure interests ❑

2➤ Describe this person to a partner or to the class. Talk about the challenges he or she has met.

PREPARING TO READ

Thinking about the topic

1➤ In this text, you will read about the living conditions of the elderly in the United States. Before you read, respond to the following statements about elderly people *in your country*. Use a scale of 1 to 5. If you agree strongly, circle 1. If you disagree strongly, circle 5.

Most elderly people in my country . . .	Strongly agree		Neutral		Strongly disagree
a are lonely	1	2	3	4	5
b live in nursing homes	1	2	3	4	5
c have serious health problems	1	2	3	4	5
d live inactive lives	1	2	3	4	5
e have many financial worries	1	2	3	4	5
f fear death and dying	1	2	3	4	5

2➤ Compare answers with your classmates.

Speed reading

Use this text as an opportunity to practice your speed-reading skills. Before you start, review the guidelines for faster reading on page 36 in Chapter 2.

NOW READ

Now read the text "Late Adulthood." Time yourself (or your teacher will time you). When you finish, make a note of how long it took you to read the whole text. Then turn to the tasks that begin on page 88.

4   LATE ADULTHOOD

The transition to what we are here calling *late adulthood* generally occurs in our early to mid-60s. Perhaps the first thing we need to realize is that persons over the age of 65 comprise a sizable proportion of the population in the United States. More than 25.5 million Americans are in this age bracket, and the numbers are increasing by an average of 1,400 per day (Kermis, 1984; Storandt, 1983). Given the fact that people are living longer, coupled with the declining birth rates in this country, it is no surprise that the U.S. population now includes a greater percentage of people over the age of 65 than ever before. In 1940, fewer than 4,000 Americans were more than 100 years old, but by 1986, nearly 40,000 reached that milestone. And this trend should continue for some time. By the year 2020, Americans over 65 will make up nearly 20 percent of the population (Eisdorfer, 1983).

COMPENSATING FOR LOSSES

Ageism is the name given to the discrimination or negative stereotypes that are formed on the basis of age. Ageism is particularly acute in our attitudes about the elderly. One misconception about the aged is that they live in misery. Yes, there are often some miseries that have to be attended to. Sensory capacities are not what they used to be. But, as Skinner (1983) suggests, "If you cannot read, listen to book recordings. If you do not hear well, turn up the volume of your phonograph (and wear headphones to protect your neighbors)." Many cognitive abilities suffer with age, but others are developed to compensate for most losses.

ageism
a negative attitude toward individuals because of their age, often leading to discrimination

The accumulated experience of many years of living and working can more than compensate for the loss of mental speed that usually occurs in late adulthood.

Apparent memory loss may reflect more a choice of what one chooses to remember rather than an actual loss. There is no doubt that mental speed is lost, but the accumulated experience of years of living can, and often does, far outweigh any advantages of speed (Meer, 1986).

Yes, death becomes a reality. As many as 50 percent of the women in this country over 65 are widows. But many elderly people (3,000 in 1978) choose this time of their lives to marry for the first time (Kalish, 1982).

Yes, children have long since "left the nest," but they are still in touch, and now there are grandchildren with whom to interact. Moreover, the children of the elderly have themselves now reached adulthood and are more able and likely to provide support for aging parents. In fact, only about 5 percent of Americans over the age of 65 live in nursing homes, and fewer than 20 percent are unable to get around, to come and go as they please (Harris, 1975, 1983).

Yes, many individuals dread retirement, but most welcome it as an opportunity to do those things that they have planned on for years (Haynes et al., 1978). Many people over 65 become more physically active after retiring from a job where they were tied to a desk all day long.

HEALTH, LONELINESS, AND FEAR OF DYING

Although we often assume that old age brings with it the curse of poor health, a 1981 Harris survey tells us that only 21 percent of the respondents over age 65 claimed poor health to be a serious problem. That compares to 8 percent in the 18 to 54 age range and 18 percent in the 55 to 65 age range. So although health problems are more common, they are not

That the elderly fear death and face despair may be more myth than reality.

nearly as widespread or devastating as we might think. (It should also be noted that poor health among the elderly is very much related to income and educational levels. For example, 31 percent of those with incomes below $5,000 reported serious health problems.)

One of the findings of a 1975 Harris poll dispelled another myth of ageism: that old people are lonely. Eight percent claimed that they had no close person to talk to, but 5 percent of those surveyed who were younger than 65 agreed to the same statement. In short, old age is not as bad as we sometimes let ourselves believe; that is, it is not *necessarily* as bad.

To return one last time to Erikson, we find that his final stage of psychosocial development is reserved for this period beyond the age of 65. According to Erikson, it is at this stage that it is common for individuals to pause and reflect on their lives, what they have accomplished, the mark they have left, and what they might do with the time remaining. If all goes well with this self-examination, the individual develops a sense of **ego identity** – a sense of wholeness, an acceptance that all is well and can only get better. If self-examination results in regret, if life seems unfulfilled, with choices badly made, then one may face despair and turn only to death.

Although elderly people may have to deal with dying and death, they are generally less morbid about it than are adolescents (Lanetto, 1980). In one study (Kalish and Reynolds, 1976), adults over 60 did more frequently think about and talk about death than did younger adults surveyed. However, of all the adults in the study, the oldest group expressed the least fear of death, some even saying they were eager for it.

Many elderly people lead active and fulfilling lives well into late adulthood.

AFTER YOU READ

Time it took to read the text: _____ (to the nearest tenth of a minute, for example, 3.4 minutes).

Task 1 Reading for detail

Test your understanding of this text by answering these multiple-choice reading comprehension questions without looking back at the text. Choose the best answer from the choices listed.

1 A good title for this text would be _____.
   a The Myths of Old Age
   b The Misery of Old Age
   c The Joys of Old Age

2 The percentage of elderly people in the American population is increasing because _____.
   a people are living longer
   b couples are having fewer children
   c both a and b

3 Which of the following may not actually be lost in old age, although it often appears to be?
   a hearing
   b memory
   c mental speed

4 One advantage of being elderly that is mentioned in this text is that the elderly _____.
   a can look forward to the excitement of remarriage
   b can afford to pay people to look after them
   c often have children who can give them financial and practical support

5 What percentage of people over 65 in America live in special nursing homes for the aged?
   a 5 percent
   b 20 percent
   c 40 percent

6 According to the text, it is not unusual for people who have had desk jobs to _____ after they retire.
   a develop serious health problems
   b take up sedentary hobbies (hobbies you do while sitting)
   c become much more active

7 Approximately _____ of people over 65 in America say that they have a serious health problem.

   a 5 percent

   b 20 percent

   c 40 percent

8 When the number of people over 65 who say they are lonely is compared with the number of people under 65 who say the same thing, we find that _____.

   a the number is approximately the same

   b many more people over 65 claim to be lonely

   c many more people under 65 claim to be lonely

9 Erikson states that in late adulthood we examine our lives and may develop a sense of ego identity. This happens when _____.

   a we feel badly about our lives and wish we had made better decisions

   b we feel good about our lives and look to the future with optimism

   c all we can think about is that we must face death

10 Which of the following statements about elderly people and death is true?

   a They tend to think about death less than young adults.

   b They tend to be less afraid of dying than young adults.

   c They tend to talk about death less frequently than young adults.

Follow-up: How well did you read?

1➤ Reread the text and check your answers to the reading comprehension questions.

2➤ Fill in the box to calculate your reading speed in words per minute (wpm) and your percent correct on the reading comprehension questions. A good goal would be to read at about 250 wpm with an accuracy of 70 percent.

a time to read _____
b number of words _____ 871 _____
c wpm (*b/a*) _____
d number correct _____
e percent correct (*d* x 10) _____

Task 2 Reading critically

> **J**ust because an argument is in print in a book or newspaper article does not mean it is always true. When you read, you should read critically, that is, you should develop the habit of assessing whether what you are reading is logical or could be looked at in a different way.

The following six myths are attacked in this text.

1 The elderly are lonely.
2 The elderly live in nursing homes.
3 The elderly have serious health problems.
4 The elderly live inactive lives.
5 The elderly have many financial worries.
6 The elderly fear death and dying.

With a partner, find the arguments used in the text to show that these are myths and assess how strong those arguments are. Can you think of facts that the author did not write about, which might show late adulthood in a less positive light?

Task 3 Writing a summary

Read through the text again and write a one-paragraph summary pointing out the myths that exist about old age. Remember to include only the most important information.

CHAPTER 4 Writing assignment

Choose one of the following topics as your chapter writing assignment.

1 Contrast what you have learned in this chapter about marriage and family life in the United States with conditions in your country.

2 Contrast what you have learned about the living conditions, physical health, and state of mind of the elderly in the United States with those of the elderly in your country.

3 Choose one of the three periods of adulthood – early, middle, or late – and explain why you think that period is the best part of adult life. In your argument, be sure to explain why you did not choose either of the other two periods.

UNIT 3

Intelligence

In this unit we study issues surrounding the topic of intelligence. In Chapter 5, we see that although intelligence is difficult to define, psychologists have been trying to measure it in different ways for a long time. In Chapter 6, we study one of the oldest questions in psychology, known as the "nature versus nurture" debate: Is it in our genetic makeup (nature) to reach a certain level of intelligence, or does environment (nurture) play a more important role?

PREVIEWING THE UNIT

> **B**efore reading a unit (or chapter) of a textbook, it is a good idea to preview the contents page and think about the topics that will be covered.

Read the contents page for Unit 3 and answer the following questions with a partner.

Chapter 5: Assessing intelligence

1► In the first three sections of Chapter 5, you will read about how a person's intelligence can be assessed. Look at the graph in Figure A and answer these questions:

1 What does this graph describe?

2 What does it mean if you have an IQ score of 100? Of 155? Of 55?

3 Are intelligence tests commonly given in your country? Have you ever had your intelligence tested? Do you know your IQ score?

2► In the final section of this chapter, you will read about a study of American children with very high IQs. Such children often have a rather negative stereotype in the United States. What stereotype do you have of the "brainy child" in your country? How accurate do you think it is?

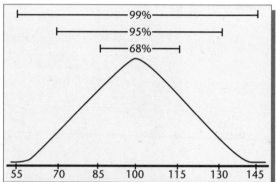

Figure A   Distribution of IQ scores in the general population

Chapter 6: Accounting for variations in intelligence

1► In the first two sections of this chapter, you will read about differences in intelligence between men and women, and between the old and the young. Make a prediction as to whether the following two statements are going to be true or false.

_____ *1* On average, women do better than men on tests of general intellectual ability.
_____ *2* On average, people in their twenties do better on IQ tests than people in their fifties.

2► The final two sections in Chapter 6 focus on the opening question to Section 3: "Are the differences we observe in intelligence due to heredity (nature) or to environmental influences (nurture)?" What do you think the answer is? Choose one of the following:

1 Differences in intelligence are mostly due to heredity.

2 Differences in intelligence are mostly due to the environment.

3 Differences in intelligence are due equally to heredity and the environment.

4 This will always be an impossible question to answer.

UNIT CONTENTS

PREPARING TO READ

Thinking about the topic

Whom do you know who is more or less intelligent than you? Your brother? Sister? Parents? Friends? What does it mean to say that someone is more or less intelligent than someone else? What do we mean by intelligence?

1➤ Work with a partner and write down four factors by which you judge someone to be intelligent or not.

1 _____

2 _____

3 _____

4 _____

2➤ Compare answers with another pair of students.

Skimming for main ideas

Skim through the text and find the paragraph that deals with each of the following topics. Write the number of the paragraph in the blank.

_____ *a* Some problems with the theoretical definition of intelligence
_____ *b* An operational definition of intelligence
_____ *c* Several common-sense definitions of intelligence
_____ *d* A theoretical definition of intelligence

NOW READ

Now read the text "Intelligence Defined." When you finish, turn to the tasks on page 97.

CHAPTER 5

Assessing Intelligence

---

1   INTELLIGENCE DEFINED

Intelligence has been defined in many different ways. Some have defined 1
it as the sum total of everything you know, others have defined it as the
ability to learn and profit from experience, still others define it as the
ability to solve problems. Of course, there is nothing wrong with any of
these definitions of intelligence. The problem is that not one of them
alone seems to say it all. We use the term *intelligence* so often as a general label for so many abilities, that it is now almost impossible to give it a
specific definition.

However, it is important that we decide on a definition to guide us 2
through this chapter. We suggest, therefore, that we accept two definitions, one academic and theoretical, the other operational and practical.
For our theoretical definition of intelligence we can do no better than
David Wechsler, who defines it as "the capacity of an individual to
understand the world about him (or her) and his (or her) resourcefulness
to cope with its challenges" (1975).

This definition, and others like it, does present some ambiguities. Just 3
what does one mean by "capacity"? What is actually meant by "understand the world"? What if the world never really challenges one's resourcefulness? Will such people be less intelligent? What at first may seem like

Teachers, like the rest of us, are continually making judgments about a person's intelligence, although it is difficult to define.

a very sensible and inclusive definition of intelligence may, upon reflection, pose even more definitional problems.

4   One way to overcome these difficulties is to define the concept of intelligence operationally. Thus, we can operationally define intelligence as that which intelligence tests measure. Notice that this definition sidesteps the thorny conceptual problem of coming to grips with the "true" nature of intelligence; it doesn't solve it. But it does what most operational definitions do – it gives a definition we can work with for a while. To use this definition, then, we need to see how intelligence tests work. We will then be able to see how people differ in terms of intelligence.

AFTER YOU READ

Task 1 Reading for detail

Answer the following questions and then compare your answers with a partner.

1 In paragraph 1, how many definitions of *intelligence* are there? How many of these definitions were similar to your ideas in your prereading discussion?

2 In paragraphs 2 and 3, what would you say is the author's attitude toward Wechsler's definition of intelligence? (Choose one.)

   a It must be rejected, because it is too ambiguous.

   b It has problems, but it is as good as any other.

   c It poses more definitional problems than it solves.

   d It is a very sensible and inclusive definition.

3 In paragraph 4, what is the operational definition of intelligence?

Task 2 Building vocabulary: Collocations

> When studying vocabulary, it is always a good idea to be aware of collocations, such as nouns that frequently combine in object position with certain verbs or verb phrases.

1➤ Scan the text and find the nouns that occur in object position with these verbs.

to learn from _____   to present_____

to solve _____   to pose _____

to cope with_____   to overcome _____

2➤ Look at these collocations for the noun *problem*. Draw a line from each collocation in column A to its near synonym in column B.

A	B
to attack a problem	to confront a problem
to face a problem	to tackle a problem
to solve a problem	to be posed with a problem
to have a problem	to overcome a problem

3➤ Complete the following short text with verbs that collocate with *problem*.

Imagine you _____ a problem. It is no good running away from that problem. You must _____ the problem and really_____ it. Hopefully, in the end you will then_____ your problem.

PREPARING TO READ

Examining graphic material

1➤ Study the diagram in Figure B, which shows the components of a well-known intelligence test, the Stanford-Binet. A subject's general intelligence score is determined by testing his or her crystallized abilities (verbal and quantitative reasoning); fluid-analytic abilities (abstract/visual reasoning) and short-term memory. These abilities are tested on fifteen subtests.

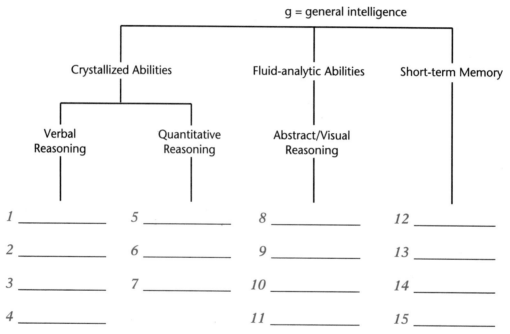

Figure B The factors tested by the Stanford-Binet, Fourth Edition

2➤ Look at Figure 5.1 on page 99 and carefully read the descriptions of the fifteen subtests. With a partner work out answers to the following, and write your answers into the diagram above.

1 Which four subtests test verbal reasoning?
2 Which three subtests test quantitative reasoning?
3 Which four subtests test abstract/visual reasoning?
4 Which four subtests test short-term memory?

NOW READ

Now read the text "The Stanford-Binet Intelligence Test." When you finish, turn to the tasks on page 101.

2   THE STANFORD-BINET INTELLIGENCE TEST

Alfred Binet (1857–1911) was the leading psychologist in France at the turn of the century. Binet worked at the psychology laboratory at the Sorbonne. He studied hypnosis, abnormal behaviors, optical illusions, and thinking processes, but by far his major concern was with individual differences. In particular, Binet was curious about how people differed in their ability to solve problems.

It was not surprising then that Binet was asked in 1900 to investigate why it was that some children in the Paris school system were unable to benefit from the educational experiences that they were given. What was the problem? Were the children uninterested? Did they have emotional problems? Or were they just intellectually incapable of grasping and making use of the educational material with which they were presented? In studying this problem, Binet decided to try to construct a test to measure the intellectual abilities of children.

Alfred Binet

Binet's first test appeared in 1905 and was revised in 1908. The test was an immediate success, and it caught the attention of Lewis M. Terman at Stanford University, who translated it into English and supervised a revision in 1916. It then became known as the Stanford-Binet test. Since then, it has undergone a number of revisions, the most recent of which was published in 1986.

---

1. **Vocabulary.** For ages 2–6, provide name and definition of picture of object; for older subjects, define words increasing in difficulty
2. **Bead memory.** String a series of multicolored beads after seeing a picture of the required string
3. **Quantitative.** Complete a series of arithmetic problems, from simple counting to complex word problems
4. **Memory for sentences.** Repeat a series of sentences of increasing complexity
5. **Pattern analysis.** At young ages, match shapes to holes; at older levels, use blocks of different designs to copy patterns of increasing complexity
6. **Comprehension.** Answer questions like, "Why does the government regulate radio and television broadcasts?"
7. **Absurdities.** Identify what is wrong with picture: for example, a wagon with triangular wheels
8. **Memory for digits.** Repeat a list of digits of increasing length; forwards or backwards
9. **Copying.** Draw (duplicate) a series of geometric line drawings of increasing complexity
10. **Memory for objects.** Recognize a series of pictures of simple objects presented one at a time from a larger picture displaying many objects
11. **Matrices.** Shown a series of pictures, determine which of a number of alternatives comes next in the series
12. **Number series.** Presented with a series of numbers, determine what number comes next
13. **Paper folding and cutting.** Fold and/or cut a sheet of paper according to a prescribed pattern
14. **Verbal relations.** Given three words that are alike and a fourth that is different, explain why the three are alike and the fourth is different
15. **Equation building.** Given a series of digits and algebraic signs (+, x, -), create a balanced equation

Figure 5.1 The fifteen subtests of the 1986 edition of the Stanford-Binet Intelligence Scale

Figure 5.2 An idealized curve showing the distribution of scores on the Stanford-Binet if it were taken by a large sample of the general population. *The numbers at the top of the curve indicate the percentage of the population expected to score within the indicated range (i.e., 68 percent score between 85 and 115; 95 percent between 70 and 130; and 99 percent between 55 and 145).*

crystallized abilities
abilities needed to acquire and use information; thought to be fostered by formal education

fluid–analytic abilities
abilities that enable an individual to gain insight into complex problems, especially figural and nonverbal problems; thought to develop independently of formal schooling

standard age score (SAS)
a score on an intelligence test, by which one's performance is compared to others of the same age; a score of 100 is average

So what is this test like? The 1986 edition of the Stanford-Binet is quite different from its predecessors. Subjects are tested on three different types of abilities (see Figure B in "Preparing to Read"). **Crystallized abilities** are defined as those needed to acquire and use verbal and quantitative concepts to solve problems. They are influenced by schooling and could be called "an academic ability" factor. **Fluid-analytic abilities** are skills needed to solve problems that involve figural or nonverbal types of information. These skills are thought to be not so influenced by formal schooling. Essentially, they involve the ability to see things in new and different ways. The third factor is *short-term memory*.

There are 15 subtests that test the three abilities (see Figure 5.1). Within each of these subtests, the items are arranged by difficulty, which is determined by appropriate age level. Age levels vary from 2 years old to adult (18+). This means that if you were giving the test to an eight-year-old, you would probably start by giving items for a six-year-old and then continue to more difficult test items, until the child consistently fails to answer questions.

In interpreting an individual's scores, one compares the scores to those earned by children of the same age. The resulting score is called a **standard age score** or **SAS**. Standard age scores are always computed so that an average SAS always comes out to be 100. People who do better than average have standard age scores above 100 and those who perform less well than others their age have standard age scores below 100. Figure 5.2 shows the way that SASs on the Stanford-Binet are distributed for the general population.

The Stanford-Binet has been in use for a long time. There is much to be said for it. It is a well-recognized measure of those behaviors that we commonly label intelligent, at least in an educational or academic sense – and is in this way, at least, a valid instrument. The test does have some drawbacks. It is an individual test (one subject and one examiner) and should be administered and interpreted by trained professionals. The test may take longer than an hour to administer, and hence it is quite expensive.

AFTER YOU READ

Task 1 Effective note-taking

> **H**ere are some guidelines for effective note-taking in a notebook:
> - Use abbreviations and symbols, but make sure you will know what they mean when you look at them later.
> - Do not crowd your notes. Make them easy to read by leaving plenty of space around them.
> - Make sure main points stand out by: 1) underlining and numbering them; 2) indenting lower-level details, as in an outline; 3) leaving space between each main point.
> - Write legibly.

1➤ Look at these notes for the first four paragraphs of the text. The two main points are numbered. Work with a partner. Without looking back at the text, and working from these notes only, summarize orally one main point each.

THE STANFORD-BINET INTELLIGENCE TEST
1. History of S-B
    Alfred Binet (1857–1911) Fr. psych.
        int. in individ diffs
        esp how people solve probs
        investigated Paris sch. syst.
        why some studs do well, others not
        constructed test to measure intell.
        1st test – 1905. Revised 1908
    Lewis Terman – Stanford U. prof.
        trans. t. into Eng.
        revised t. in 1916

known as Stanford-Binet
latest revision 1986

2. Factors tested in 1986 S-B
        Crystallized abilities
            verbal + quantitative skills
            influenced by schooling
            ∴ academic skill factor
        Fluid-analytic abils
            figural + nonverbal skills
            not so influenced by schooling
        Short-term memory

2➤ Take your own notes for the rest of the text.

3➤ Looking at your notes only, work with a partner and summarize orally one main point each.

Task 2 Test-taking: Preparing for a short-answer quiz

1➤ Look at your notes and write down four short-answer questions a professor might ask about this text. (See Task 3 on page 8 in Chapter 1 for information about different types of short–answer questions.)

2➤ Ask a classmate to answer these questions orally.

PREPARING TO READ

Building background knowledge on the topic

> The more you know about a topic, the easier it is to process new information from a reading.

David Wechsler designed several intelligence tests that are widely used in the United States. Subtests in the Wechsler intelligence tests are divided into two categories, or scales: a *verbal scale* and a *performance scale*. Subtests belonging to the performance scale are particularly useful when testing children who have difficulty hearing, are not fluent in the tester's language, or have trouble following classroom directions.

The five test items in Figure C are examples of items from the five different performance subtests in the Wechsler tests. Read the description of the five performance subtests in Figure 5.3 in the text, then match each of the five test items below to one of the performance subtests.

Put the panels into a meaningful order.

Put this puzzle together.

Code

Test

Using the key at the top, fill in the appropriate symbol beneath each number.

Supply the missing feature.

Copy the design shown, using another set of blocks.

Figure C   Sample performance tasks on the Wechsler tests (from Wade and Tavris, 1989)

NOW READ

Now read the text "The Wechsler Intelligence Tests." When you finish, turn to the tasks on page 105.

3 THE WECHSLER INTELLIGENCE TESTS

David Wechsler published his first general intelligence test in 1939. Unlike the version of the Stanford-Binet that existed at the time, it was designed for use with adult populations and to reduce the heavy reliance on verbal skills. With a major revision in 1955, the test became known as the Wechsler Adult Intelligence Scale (WAIS). The latest revision (now called the WAIS-R) was published in 1981. The WAIS-R is appropriate for subjects between 16 and 74 years of age and is reported to be the most commonly used of all tests in clinical practice.

A natural extension of the WAIS was the Wechsler Intelligence Scale for Children (WISC), originally published eleven years after the WAIS. After a major revision in 1974, it became known as the WISC-R. The

Verbal Scale	
Information	*(29 items)* Questions designed to tap one's general knowledge about a variety of topics dealing with one's culture, e.g., "Who wrote Huckleberry Finn?" or "How many nickels in a quarter?"
Digit span	*(7 series)* Subject is read a series of 3 to 9 digits and is asked to repeat them; then a different series is to be repeated in reverse order.
Comprehension	*(16 items)* A test of judgement, common sense, and practical knowledge, e.g., "Why is it good to have prisons?"
Similarities	*(14 pairs)* Subject must indicate the way(s) in which two things are alike, e.g., "In what way are an apple and a potato alike?"
Vocabulary	*(35 words)* Subject must provide an acceptable definition for a series of words.
Arithmetic	*(14 problems)* Math problems must be solved without the use of paper and pencil, e.g., "How far will a bird travel in 90 minutes if it flies at the rate of 10 miles per hour?"
Performance scale	
Picture completion	*(20 pictures)* Subject must identify or name the missing part or object in a drawing, e.g., a truck with only three wheels.
Picture arrangement	*(10 series)* A series of cartoonlike pictures must be arranged in an order so that they tell a story.
Block design	*(9 items)* Using blocks whose sides are either all red, all white, or diagonally red and white, subject must copy a designed picture or pattern shown on a card.
Object assembly	*(4 objects)* Free-form jigsaw puzzles must be put together to form familiar objects.
Digit symbol	In a key, each of nine digits is paired with a simple symbol. Given a random series of digits, the subject must provide the paired symbol within a time limit.

Figure 5.3 The subtests of the Wechsler Adult Intelligence Scale – Revised (WAIS-R)

A child attempts one of the performance tests in the WISC-R.

WISC-R is appropriate for testing children between the ages of 6 and 17 (there is some overlap with the WAIS). A third test in the Wechsler series is designed for younger children between the ages of 4 and 6 1/2. It is called the Wechsler Preschool and Primary Scale of Intelligence, or WPPSI. It was first published in 1967 (and is under revision). There are some subtle differences among the three Wechsler tests, but each is based on the same general logic. Therefore, we will consider only one, the WAIS-R, in any detail.

The WAIS-R is made up of eleven subtests, or scales. The subtests of the WAIS-R are arranged by the type of ability or skill being tested. The subtests are organized into two categories. Six subtests define the *verbal scale*, and five subtests constitute a *performance scale*. Figure 5.3 lists the different subtests of the WAIS-R and describes some of the sorts of items found on each. With each of the Wechsler tests, we can compute three scores: a verbal score, a performance score, and a total (or full-scale) score. As with the Stanford-Binet, the total score can be taken as an approximation of **g**, or general intellectual ability.

To administer the WAIS-R, you present each of the eleven subtests to your subject. The items within each subtest are arranged in order of difficulty. You start with relatively easy items – those you are confident that your examinee will respond to correctly – and then you progress to more difficult ones. You stop administering any one subtest when your subject fails a specified number of items in a row. You alternate between verbal and performance subtests. The whole process takes up to an hour and a half.

g-score
a measure of one's overall, general intellectual abilities, commonly thought of as IQ

AFTER YOU READ

Task 1 Reading for detail

Decide if the following statements are true (T) or false (F), according to this text.

_____ 1 The 1939 Stanford-Binet test was designed for children.

_____ 2 The WAIS-R test is a widely used intelligence test.

_____ 3 The WISC was published in 1966.

_____ 4 To test a 4-year-old child, you would use the WISC-R.

_____ 5 The three tests – the WAIS-R, the WISC-R, and the WPPSI – are designed very differently.

_____ 6 The WAIS-R has eleven subtests, which belong to two main categories.

_____ 7 While taking the WAIS-R, subjects are given the most difficult items on each subtest first.

_____ 8 Subjects take all the verbal subtests first and then all the performance subtests.

Task 2 Applying what you read: Designing a test

1➤ Look back at Figure 5.3 in the text and read the descriptions and examples given for each of the six subtests in the verbal scale. Working in groups, design several test items of your own for each of these subtests, using the guidelines below. You will also need to work out a scoring system for your test.

1 Information	Think of a few general knowledge questions for which people from any culture should know the answers.	
2 Digit span	Have subjects repeat one or two sets of digits. Have subjects also repeat one or two sets of digits in reverse order.	
3 Comprehension	Think of a question similar to the one in the example. Give subjects a time limit for answering, for example, one minute. Give different scores depending on how good you think the answer is.	
4 Similarities	Think of two things to compare. Give subjects a time limit for answering, for example, 30 seconds. The more points of comparison the subject thinks of, the higher the score.	
5 Vocabulary	Think of a short list of words for subjects to define. Make some of the words fairly common and some less common. Decide what is needed for a complete definition. The more complete the subject's definition, the higher the score. Give a time limit.	
6 Arithmetic	Think of two problems similar to the one in the example. Decide on an appropriate time limit. Remember these are to be done in the subject's head, not on paper.	

2➤ When your test is complete, pair up with a student from a different group and administer your tests to each other.

PREPARING TO READ

Thinking about the topic

We often think of gifted children as those who do well on intelligence tests. However, as you will read in this text on giftedness, there are many other ways to be gifted. Look at the pictures below and think about how else a person may be gifted.

Speed Reading

Use this text as an opportunity to practice your speed-reading skills. Before you start, review the guidelines for faster reading on page 36 in Chapter 2.

NOW READ

Now read the text "Giftedness." Time yourself (or your teacher will time you). When you finish, make a note of how long it took you to read the whole text. Then turn to the tasks that begin on page 109.

4 GIFTEDNESS

There are many ways in which a person can be gifted. A United States Office of Education report (1972) defines giftedness as a demonstrated achievement or aptitude for excellence in any one of six areas:

1 *Psychomotor ability* This is one of the most overlooked areas in which some individuals can clearly excel. We are dealing here with people of outstanding abilities in skills that require agility, strength, speed, quickness, coordination, and the like.

2 *Visual and performing arts* Some people, even as children, demonstrate an unusual talent for art, music, drama, or writing.

3 *Leadership ability* Leadership skills are valued in most societies, and there seem to be individuals who are particularly gifted in this area. This is often true even with very young children. Youngsters with good leadership skills tend to be intellectually bright, but they are not necessarily the smartest of the group.

4 *Creative or productive thinking* This area of giftedness has received considerable attention over the past 25 years. Here we are talking about individuals who may be intellectually or academically above average, but, again, not necessarily so. Among other things, people with this type of giftedness are able to generate unique and different solutions to problems.

5 *Specific academic aptitude* In this case, we are talking about people who have a flair or a special ability for a particular subject or two. Someone who is a real whiz in math, history, or laboratory science, without necessarily being outstanding in other academic areas, would fit this category.

6 *Intellectually gifted* Inclusion in this group is based on scores earned on a general intelligence test, usually a Wechsler test or the Stanford-Binet intelligence scale. It is most likely that when people use the term **mentally gifted**, they are referring to individuals who would fit this category – people of exceptionally high IQ. (IQ scores of 130 or above usually qualify for inclusion in this category. Some prefer to reserve the label for those with IQs above 135. In either case, we are dealing with a very small portion of the population – fewer than three percent qualify.)

mentally gifted
a term usually used to describe people who score 130 or higher on an IQ test

THE TERMAN STUDY

How can we describe intellectually gifted individuals? Most of what we know about the mentally gifted comes directly, or indirectly, from a classic study begun by L. M. Terman in the early 1920s. This is the same Terman who revised Binet's IQ test in 1916. Terman supervised the testing of more than a quarter of a million children throughout California. Terman's research group at Stanford University focused its attention on

The image of people with high IQ's as skinny, unathletic, unattractive, and boring is a stereotype, not a reality.

those children who earned the highest scores – about 1,500 in all, each with an IQ above 135.

Lewis Terman died in 1956, but the study of those mentally gifted individuals – who were between the ages of 8 and 12 in 1922 – still continues. Ever since their inclusion in the original study, and at regular intervals, they have been retested, surveyed, interviewed, and polled by psychologists still at Stanford. The Terman study has its drawbacks – choosing a very narrow definition of gifted in terms of IQ alone is an obvious one. Failing to control for factors such as socioeconomic level or parents' educational level is another. Nonetheless, the study is an impressive one for having been continued for more than 60 years, if nothing else. What can this longitudinal analysis tell us about people with very high IQs?

Most of Terman's results fly in the face of the common stereotype of the bright child as being skinny, anxious, clumsy, of poor health, and almost certainly wearing thick glasses. The data just do not support the stereotype. In fact, if there is any overall conclusion that might be drawn from the Terman-Stanford study, it is that, in general, gifted children experience advantages in virtually everything. They are taller, faster, better coordinated, have better eyesight, fewer emotional problems, and tend to stay married longer than average. These findings have been confirmed by others. All sorts of obvious things are also true of this sample of bright children, now oldsters. They received much more education, found better, higher-paying jobs, and had more intelligent children than did people of average intelligence. By now, we certainly know better than to overgeneralize. Every one of Terman's children (sometimes referred to as "Termites") did not grow up to be rich and famous and live happily ever after. The truth is that many did, but not all.

AFTER YOU READ

Time it took to read the text: _____ (to the nearest tenth of a minute, for example, 3.4 minutes).

Task 1 Reading for detail

Test your understanding of the text by answering these multiple-choice reading comprehension questions without looking back at the text. Choose the best answer from the choices listed.

1 According to this text it is possible to have special skills in six areas. In order to be considered "gifted," a person must show excellence in _____.

   a at least one skill

   b at least two skills

   c all six skills

2 In order to be considered "intellectually gifted," one must have an IQ of at least _____.

   a 120

   b 130

   c 140

3 L. M. Terman started his study of the mentally gifted in the _____.

   a 1910s

   b 1920s

   c 1930s

4 How many children's IQs did Terman test?

   a more than 250,000

   b 1500

   c 150

5 How many mentally gifted children did Terman study?

   a 250,000

   b 1500

   c 150

6 The Terman study _____.

   a ended with his death in 1956

   b ended recently

   c still continues

7 One problem with the Terman study is that _____.

    a the study lasted for 60 years

    b the parents were all from the same socioeconomic level and educational backgrounds

    c Terman only defined "giftedness" as being able to score 135 or above on an IQ test

8 Terman discovered that most bright children _____.

    a were taller and faster than the average child

    b had poorer physical health than the average child

    c had more emotional problems than the average child

9 When the Terman children grew up to be adults, they usually _____.

    a found lower paying jobs than average

    b had more problems in their marriage than average

    c had more intelligent children than average

10 How many of the Terman children grew up to be rich?

    a all of them

    b many of them

    c a few of them

Follow-up: How well did you read?

1► Reread the text and check your answers to the reading comprehension questions.

2► Fill in the box to calculate your reading speed in words per minute (wpm) and your percent correct on the reading comprehension questions. A good goal would be to read at about 250 wpm with an accuracy of 70 percent.

a time to read _____

b number of words _____ 730 _____

c wpm (*b/a*) _____

d number correct _____

e percent correct (*d* x 10) _____

Task 2 Personalizing the topic

1► Look at the six areas listed here in which it is possible to achieve excellence. Number them from 1 to 6 according to your strengths and weaknesses, putting a 1 in front of your area of greatest strength and a 6 in front of your area of greatest weakness.

_____ psychomotor ability
_____ visual and performing arts
_____ leadership ability
_____ creative or productive thinking
_____ specific academic aptitude
_____ intellectually gifted

2▶ Compare lists with a partner and explain your choices for numbers 1, 2, and 6.

Task 3 Writing a summary

Read through the text again and then write a one-paragraph summary of the Terman study and its findings. Remember to include only the most important information.

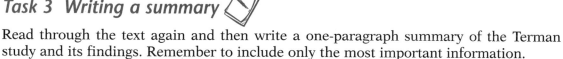

CHAPTER 5 Writing assignment

Choose one of the following topics as your chapter writing assignment.

1 To what extent do you think most education systems rely too much on intelligence tests as a measure of an individual's intelligence? Are there better ways for an education system to judge an individual?

2 When studying the text "The Wechsler Intelligence Tests," you were asked to design your own intelligence test items. Write a report on the intelligence test that you created. Describe the test items it contains, why you chose these items, the way the test was administered, and the results that you got.

3 The opening sentence of the text "Giftedness" states, "There are many ways in which a person can be gifted." In which ways are you most and least gifted? Give examples to support your answers.

PREPARING TO READ

Predicting the content

Try to predict the content of this text by filling in the grid.

Who usually does better on tests of the following skills? Check one column for each skill.	Males	Females	No difference
Speaking fluency			
Mathematical ability			
Reading			
General intelligence			
Spatial relations (mentally seeing where shapes belong)			
Fine dexterity (moving small object with your hands)			

Skimming for main ideas

Skim the text. Then put the following sentences into the correct order to create a summary of this reading.

_____ *a* Others seem to be influenced by environmental factors.

_____ *b* There is no difference between men and women in measures of global IQ.

_____ *c* Some differences seem to be due to innate factors.

_____ *d* But there are differences between men and women when specific skills are measured.

NOW READ

Now read the text "Gender and IQ" and find out how accurate your predictions were in "Predicting the Content." Then turn to the tasks on page 115.

CHAPTER 6

Accounting for Variations in Intelligence

1 GENDER AND IQ

There is a question to which we have a reasonably definitive answer: Is there a difference in measured IQ between men and women? Answer: No. At least, there are few studies that report any differences on tests of overall, general intelligence of the sort represented by an IQ score. Of course, we have to keep in mind that there may be no measurable differences between the IQs of men and women because our tests are constructed in such a way as to minimize or eliminate any such differences. Usually, if an item on an intelligence test clearly discriminates between men and women, it is dropped from consideration.

When we look beyond the global measure of an IQ score, however, there do seem to be some reliable indications of sex differences on specific intellectual skills. For example, it is generally the case that females score (on average, remember) higher than males on tests of verbal fluency, reading ability, and *fine dexterity* (the ability to manipulate small objects). Males, on the other hand, outscore females on tests of mathematical reasoning and *spatial relations*.

Tests of spatial relations require the subject to visualize and mentally manipulate figures and forms. What is curious about this rather specialized ability is that males seem to perform better than females on such tasks from an early age, widening the gap through the school years, even though this particular ability seems to be only slightly related to any academic coursework. What this means is that sex differences here cannot be easily attributed to differences in educational opportunity.

On the other hand, educational experiences may have a great deal to do with observed differences in mathematical ability. Scores on tests of mathematics and arithmetic skills are very well correlated with the num-

"How come girls are so much smarter than boys when we're kids, and then when we grow up boys get to run everything?"

ber and nature of the math classes taken while a student is in high school. For many reasons, males tend to enroll in advanced math courses at a higher rate than females. It is not surprising, then, that by the time they leave high school, there are significant differences between men and women on tests of mathematical ability. Quoting from an article by Lyle Jones (1984), who has constructed many studies of racial differences in IQ, "At age 13, for neither blacks nor whites is there any evidence for a mean (average) sex difference in mathematics achievement. . . . At age 17, for both blacks and whites, the mean for males is significantly higher than for females. . . ."

So it seems that any differences that can be found between males and females on intellectual tasks are reasonably small, quite specific, and probably due to environmental influences and schooling experiences – although on this last conclusion, all the data are not yet in.

AFTER YOU READ

Task 1 Understanding the organization of a text

> A text often starts out with an introduction that contains a statement to be proven. It may then continue with paragraphs that provide evidence in support of that statement and end with a conclusion that assesses the strength of the evidence given. This structure is often held together by signal words and phrases that remind you of what you have already read and are about to read. Look out for these signal words and phrases that help guide you through a text.

1➤ Without looking back at the text that you have just read, number the following short passages in the order that they appear in the text.

_____ a *What this means is that* sex differences here cannot be easily attributed to differences in educational opportunity.

_____ b *So it seems that* any differences that can be found between males and females on intellectual tasks are reasonably small, quite specific and probably due to environmental influences. . . .

_____ c There is a question to which we have a reasonably definitive answer: Is there a difference in measured IQ between men and women? Answer: No. *At least . . .*

_____ d *On the other hand,* educational experiences may have a great deal to do with observed differences in mathematical ability.

_____ e When we look beyond the global measure of an IQ score, *however,* there do seem to be some reliable indications of sex differences on specific intellectual skills. *For example . . .*

2➤ Compare your answers with a partner, and explain how the words in italics guide the reader through the text. In each case, discuss how the particular word or phrase tells you about what you have just read, are about to read, or in some cases both.

Task 2 Reading for detail

1➤ According to this text, differences between men and women have been noted in the following skills. Which differences seem to be due to environmental factors (write **ENV** in the blank) and which seem to be due to innate factors (write **INN** in the blank)? If no explanation is given, leave the blank empty.

_____ 1 reading
_____ 2 math
_____ 3 verbal fluency
_____ 4 fine dexterity
_____ 5 spatial relations

2➤ Compare your answers with a partner. Find the parts of the text which led you to your answers.

PREPARING TO READ

Understanding statistical terms

In academic reading, you will often come across statistical terms, so it is important to be familiar with the most common ones. One of the most basic statistical terms is *correlation*. A correlation tells you how closely two events or conditions (often called *variables*) are related. The highest possible correlation is 1.0, which means that every time that one condition or event is present, the other is also. Lower levels of correlation range from 0.9 downwards. Scientists are often looking for significant or high correlations in their research because a high correlation suggests that there may be a causal relationship between two variables.

Study Figure 6.1 in the text and answer the following questions.

1 What is being correlated?
2 According to this graph, is there a high correlation? A low correlation?
3 Describe how you think the data were collected for this graph.

Skimming for main ideas

1➤ Skim through the text and find the paragraph in which each of the following appears. Write the number of the paragraph in the blanks.

_____ *a* data about IQ scores gathered using a cross-sectional method
_____ *b* an example to show why the best answer to questions about IQ and age is "It depends"
_____ *c* a definition of the longitudinal method of gathering data
_____ *d* a discussion about the usefulness of giving IQ tests to young children
_____ *e* definitions of fluid intelligence and crystallized intelligence
_____ *f* a comparison of the IQ scores of young children with their adult IQ scores

2➤ Compare answers with a partner.

NOW READ

Now read the text "Age Differences and IQ." When you finish, turn to the tasks that begin on page 119.

2 AGE DIFFERENCES AND IQ

You know a great deal more now than you did when you were 12 years *1*
old. You knew more when you were 12 than you did when you were 10.
You learned a lot in fifth and sixth grades. In fact, when you were 12, you
probably believed that you knew more than your parents did! Certainly
what we know generally increases with age, but what we "know" is not
a direct measure of intelligence.

One interesting question is whether the IQ scores of young children *2*
can predict their IQ scores at ages 14 or 40 or 80. As it happens, the measured IQs of individuals much younger than 7 do not correlate very well
with later IQ scores. We cannot put too much importance on IQs earned
by 4-year-olds as predictors of adult intellectual abilities. The data in
Figure 6.1 are typical in this regard. They show the correlations of IQ
scores earned at ages 16 to 18 with IQ scores at some younger age. Notice
that when previous testing was done before 7 or 8 years of age, the correlations are quite low.

This does not mean that the testing of young children is without pur- *3*
pose. Determining the intellectual abilities of young children is often
very useful, particularly if there is some concern about retardation or if
there is some thought that the child may be exceptional or gifted. The
resulting scores may not predict adult intelligence well, but they do
serve as a guide to assess the development of the child compared to
other children. Even taken as a rough guide or indicator, knowing as
early as possible that there may be some intellectual problem with a
youngster is useful information.

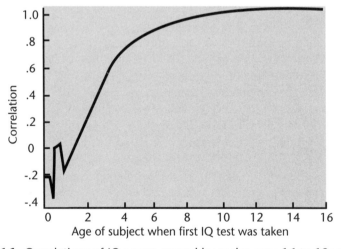

Figure 6.1 Correlations of IQ scores earned by males ages 16 to 18 with IQ
scores earned at a younger age by the same subjects (from Bayley
and Schaefer, 1964)

How does an individual's intelligence change over a lifetime?

cross–sectional method
a research method in which many subjects of different ages are compared on some measure at roughly the same time

longitudinal method
a research method in which measures are taken on the same subjects repeatedly over time

4   What about intellectual changes throughout one's whole life span? Does intelligence decrease with age? Perhaps you can anticipate the answer: yes, no, and it depends. Much of the data that we have on age differences in IQ scores have been gathered using a **cross-sectional method**. That is, IQ tests are given at roughly the same time to a large number of subjects of different ages. When that is done, the results seem to indicate that overall, global IQ peaks in the early 20s, stays rather stable for about 20 years, and then declines rather sharply.

5   A different approach to the same question would be to test the same individuals over a long period of time. This is the **longitudinal method**. When this technique is used, things don't look quite the same, usually showing IQ scores rising until the mid-50s and then very gradually declining.

6   So we have a qualified "yes" and a qualified "no" as answers to our questions about age and IQ so far. Probably the best answer is "It depends." Some studies of cognitive abilities seem to demonstrate that we should ask about specific intellectual skills, because they do not all decline at the same rate, and some do not decline at all. For example, tests of vocabulary often show no drop in scores with increasing age whatsoever, while tests of verbal fluency often show steep declines beginning at age 30.

7   Another "it depends" answer comes to the surface when we consider the distinction between what is called *fluid intelligence* and *crystallized intelligence*. It appears that fluid intelligence – abilities that relate to speed, adaptation, flexibility, and abstract reasoning – includes the sorts of skills that show the greatest decline with age. On the other hand, crystallized intelligence – abilities that depend on acquired knowledge, accumulated experiences, and general information – includes the sorts of skills that remain quite constant or even increase throughout one's lifetime.

AFTER YOU READ

Task 1 Reading for detail

Discuss the answers to the following questions with a partner.

1 What is the youngest age at which you can test a child's IQ and closely predict the child's adult IQ?

2 Does intelligence decrease with age? The author's answer to this question is "yes," "no," and "it depends." Explain why each of these answers is possible.

3 What are the differences between collecting cross-sectional data and collecting data longitudinally?

4 Give examples to explain what you think the author means by *fluid intelligence* and *crystallized intelligence*. (Look back at the text in Section 2 of Chapter 5, "The Stanford-Binet Intelligence Test," on page 99, for additional information on this topic.)

Task 2 Building vocabulary: Subtechnical vocabulary

> Certain words and phrases occur frequently in all academic writing, regardless of the specific academic discipline. Such words are sometimes referred to as subtechnical vocabulary and are particularly important for college students to learn and be able to use.

1➤ The following words occur in the text. Each of them may be used to describe changes in numerical data over time. Put each word into the correct column, depending on whether it describes an upward change or a downward change.*

decline   decrease   increase
rise   peak   drop

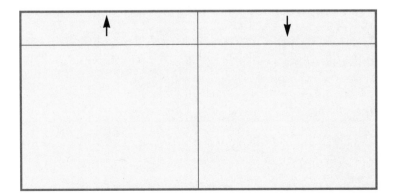

*Note that the expressions in the text *remain constant* and *stay stable* are both terms that mean that things stay the same, in other words, that is there is no movement up or down.

2▸ The words *gradual(ly)*, *sharp(ly)*, *steady* (or *steadily*), *steep(ly)*, and *sudden(ly)* are often found accompanying the six words listed in step 1 of this task. These words tell whether the movement up or down is fast or slow. Put each one into the appropriate column, depending on which meaning it has.

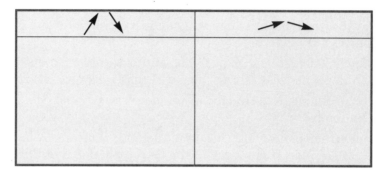

Task 3 Turning written text into a graphic

> **W**ritten information can often be made clearer with a chart, diagram, or graph. When possible, create one of these visual aids to illustrate what you have read, and include it in your notes.

This graph was created from the description in paragraph 4 of how global IQ scores change with age when gathered using a cross-sectional method.

Global IQ scores (cross–sectional method)

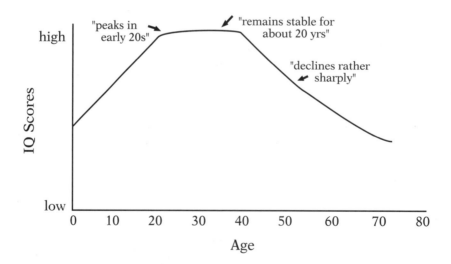

1▸ Make similar graphs to illustrate the other changes in test scores described in this text. (Assume a steep rise in all measures from ages 0 to 20.)

Vocabulary test scores

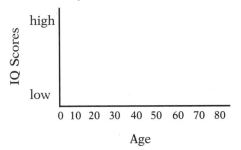

Crystallized intelligence scores

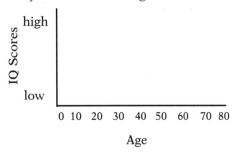

Tests of verbal fluency

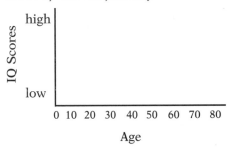

Fluid intelligence scores

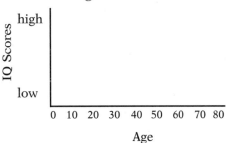

Global IQ scores (longitudinal method)

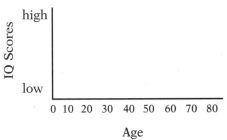

2▸ Compare your graphs with a partner.

Task 4 Writing: Turning a graph into text

> **W**hen taking a test or writing a paper, you may have to write about information that appears in a graphic format. This is a skill that you need to practice and develop.

Choose one of the graphs that you have just created and, without looking back at the text, write a description of what it shows.

PREPARING TO READ

Thinking about the topic

> "Are the differences we observe in intelligence due to heredity (nature) or to environmental influences (nurture)?"

This is the opening question in this section. Imagine that you are a psychologist studying differences in intelligence. Working with a few of your classmates, design the perfect experiment involving twins to determine which is a more important influence on intelligence – heredity or environment.

Building vocabulary: Guessing meaning from context

> **D**o not look up every unfamiliar word in the dictionary. Get into the habit of guessing meaning from context.

Read these passages from the text and use the context to guess what the words in bold probably mean.

> We could take individuals with exactly the same **genetic constitution** (that is, **identical** twins) and **raise** them in different environments. Or we could take people of clearly different genetic constitutions and raise them in identical environments.

genetic constitution(s) _____

identical _____

raise _____

> No matter how important we feel our scientific question is, we cannot simply **pluck** children out of their homes and then systematically **assign** them to different environmental conditions just **for the sake of** an experiment.

pluck _____

assign _____

for the sake of _____

NOW READ

Now read the text "Nature Versus Nurture." When you finish, turn to the tasks on page 125.

3 NATURE VERSUS NURTURE

Are the differences we observe in intelligence due to heredity (nature) or to environmental influences (nurture)? This is one of the oldest and most enduring questions in all of psychology. As reasonable as it may sound, the question does not have a reasonable answer. At least it has no simple, straightforward answer. As we shall see, there is some evidence that intelligence tends to run in families and may be due in part to innate, inherited factors. There are also data (and common sense) that tell us that a person's environment can and does affect intellectual, cognitive functioning. After all these years of scientific investigation, why can't we provide an answer to this question?

When we ask about the origin of intelligence, we have two large conceptual problems (and many smaller ones). We have seen that one difficulty is our inability to define intelligence to everyone's satisfaction. Unable to settle on just one definition, we usually end up relying on intelligence tests to provide operational measures of intelligence, but there continues to be substantial disagreement about the quality and the fairness of our intelligence tests (Mackintosh, 1986).

Our second major problem has to do with the limitations of research design – specifically, the inability to provide adequate controls. Just how might we determine if any trait, including intelligence, is experiential (environmental) or genetic (inherited) in origin? In theory, a couple of

After years of scientific investigation, we still do not know whether the intelligence of each of these children is more the result of their genetic inheritance or their environment.

approaches comes to mind. We could take individuals with exactly the same genetic constitution (that is, identical twins) and raise them in different environments. Or we could take people of clearly different genetic constitutions and raise them in identical environments. Either sort of experimental manipulation might prove to be very helpful in separating the two major influences on intelligence.

It doesn't take very long to figure out why such manipulations are not possible – at least with human subjects. How could we ever guarantee that any two persons were raised in identical environments? How can we ever get many more than two subjects at a time who have exactly the same genetic constitution? Even with pairs of subjects, who is to decide what kinds of environments each would be assigned? No matter how important we feel our scientific question is, we cannot simply pluck children out of their homes and then systematically assign them to different environmental conditions just for the sake of an experiment. Nor can we severely deprive children for a few years to see what cognitive abilities might develop without the benefit of a stimulating environment.

AFTER YOU READ

Task 1 Reading for detail

Look in the text for answers to the following questions. Then compare your answers with a partner.

1 What are two conflicting answers to the opening question in this text?
2 What are two conceptual problems that make the opening question difficult to answer?
3 What are two possible experiments that could be designed in order to find the answer to the opening question?
4 What are two moral objections to the two experiments that could be designed in order to find the answer to the opening question?

Task 2 Punctuation: The use of parentheses

> **P**unctuation carries meaning. Make sure you understand how punctuation is used in English. For example, parentheses, or rounded brackets, may be used in several different ways:
>
> - to add extra commentary – something the author wants to say that is of interest, but not essential to the text
> - to give a synonym – a word or phrase that is equal in meaning to the word or words just before it
> - to provide a bibliographic reference – the author and year of publication of the work from which a quotation or a piece of information was taken

Find where each example in the following list occurs in the text. If it adds commentary, place a plus sign (+) next to it. If it gives a synonym, place an equal sign (=) next to it. If it provides a bibliographic reference, write *REF.*

_____ 1 (nature)
_____ 2 (and common sense)
_____ 3 (and many smaller ones)
_____ 4 (Mackintosh, 1986)
_____ 5 (environmental)
_____ 6 (that is, identical twins)

Task 3 Writing

Choose one of the four questions in Task 1 and prepare a written answer to it.

PREPARING TO READ

Examining graphic material

> **B**efore reading a text, it is a good idea to examine any graphic material (graphs, charts, photographs, and so on).

Figure 6.2 in the text shows the average correlations of IQ scores of different subjects. Some subjects were genetically related, some were not. Some subjects were raised in the same household, others were not. When the IQs of subjects are similar, we see high correlations. When the IQ scores of subjects are very different, we see low correlations.

Working with a partner, look at the figure and answer the following questions.

The subjects
1 Under what circumstances can you imagine that twins might be raised apart?
2 Under what circumstances can you imagine that children who are unrelated might be raised together?
3 What is the difference between identical twins and fraternal twins?

The scores
4 What is the average correlation of IQ scores of identical twins raised together?
5 What is the average correlation of IQ scores of identical twins raised apart?
6 What is the average correlation of IQ scores of unrelated people who are raised apart?
7 What is the range of correlations of IQ scores of parents and their children?

Reading the conclusion to get the main idea

> **I**n a concluding paragraph, an author will often review what he or she has written. Reading the conclusion first, therefore, is often a good way to preview the main ideas of the whole text.

Before reading this text, study the concluding paragraph. Based on what you read in this paragraph, discuss with a partner what you think you will read about in the other paragraphs of this text.

NOW READ

Now read the text "The Study of Twins." When you finish, turn to the tasks that begin on page 129.

4 THE STUDY OF TWINS

Maybe we can't all agree precisely on what intelligence is, but we can use intelligence test scores as an approximation of an operational definition. Perhaps we can't do the perfectly controlled heredity/environment experiment, but we can look at the relationships among the IQs of people with similar and different genetic histories who have been reared in similar and different environments. Such data may be flawed, but perhaps they can give us some helpful leads.

As you might imagine, studies that examine the correlations of IQ test scores of persons with varying degrees of genetic similarity and those reared in similar and dissimilar environments have been done a number of times. The results of some of the better of these studies are summarized in Figure 6.2. These are oft-cited data, and we ought to be sure that we understand what they mean.

On the left side of the figure, we have a listing of the types of subjects whose IQ scores have been correlated. As you can see, as we go down the list, the genetic similarity between subjects increases from unrelated individuals reared apart to identical twins reared together. The graph shows the average (in this case the median) correlation for each of the pairs of groups named under "Subjects." These correlations represent average values from many correlational studies. Quite clearly, such data, drawn

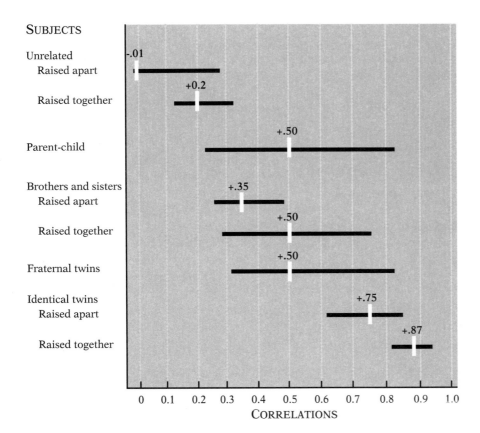

Figure 6.2 Correlations of IQ scores as a function of genetic and environmental similarity. *Vertical lines indicate average (median) correlations, and horizontal lines indicate the range of correlations from many different studies reviewed by Erlenmeyer-Kimling and Jarvik (1963).*

They look alike, they think alike! Research shows that twins usually have very similar IQs, even when they're raised in different environments.

from a number of studies conducted at different times, with different subjects, and with different intents, need to be interpreted with great caution. Even so, a few general conclusions seem reasonable.

As genetic similarities between subjects increase, correlations also increase. Correlations between the IQ scores of individuals who are unrelated in any biological sense appear quite low. Remembering that fraternal twins are just siblings who happen to be born at the same time, we find that IQs among family members in general are correlated somewhere near 0.50. When we examine the correlations of IQs of identical twins (whose genetic constitutions are the same, of course), we find very high correlations. It seems quite obvious by inspection that genetic similarity and IQ are positively correlated.

You should also notice another difference in the data presented in Figure 6.2. Regardless of genetic similarity, the correlations for subjects raised together are consistently higher than for subjects raised apart in different environments. We do need to note that children raised apart need not necessarily be reared in significantly different environments, and being raised together does not guarantee that environments are identical. What these differences do suggest is that environmental influences also affect IQ scores. Even though we are looking at grouped data, and even though many factors are left uncontrolled, inheritance clearly influences intelligence as measured by IQ scores, but so does environment.

To review, the perfect experiment, or correlational study, to determine the relative importance of heredity and the environment has not yet been done. (In fact, there is an argument that suggests that it cannot be done.) From the data that we have at present, there is evidence that can be used to justify almost any rationale: that one (nature) or the other (nurture) or both are important. It does seem that, in general, IQ is strongly affected by genetic predispositions. At the same time, it is true that IQ can be influenced or modified by the environment. The more extreme the environments, the greater the resulting differences in IQs.

AFTER YOU READ

Task 1 Interpreting the data

Some of the data in Figure 6.2 and in the text support the notion that heredity is important in determining intelligence; some data support the notion that environment is important. Insert either the word *heredity* or *environment* in each blank in order to make true statements.

1 The average correlation of IQ scores of brothers and sisters raised apart is lower than the average correlation of IQ scores of brothers and sisters raised together. Therefore, _____ must play an important role in determining intelligence.

2 The average correlation of IQ scores of identical twins, regardless of whether they were raised together or apart, is higher than the average correlation of any other set of IQ scores. Therefore, _____ must play an important role in determining intelligence.

3 The average correlation of IQ scores of brothers and sisters raised apart is higher than the average correlation of IQ scores of unrelated subjects raised together. Therefore, _____ must play an important role in determining intelligence.

4 The average correlation of IQ scores of identical twins raised apart is lower than the average correlation of IQ scores of identical twins raised together. Therefore, _____ must play an important role in determining intelligence.

Task 2 Language focus: Expressing parallel change

1➤ Look at these two sentences taken from the text. They illustrate two different ways of expressing parallel change, in which a change in one factor is accompanied by a similar change in another factor. Rewrite each sentence using the sentence structure of the other sentence.

- As genetic similarities between subjects increase, correlations also increase.
- The more extreme the environments, the greater the resulting differences in IQs.

1 The more genetic similarities between subjects increase, the _____

2 As environments become more extreme, _____

2➤ Look at this sentence, also taken from the text. It illustrates a third way of expressing parallel change, using the construction *so* + auxiliary verb. Use the *so* + auxiliary verb construction to rewrite the endings to the original two sentences in step 1 of this task. Make sure that the overall meaning of the sentences does not change.

- . . . [I]nheritance clearly influences intelligence as measured by IQ scores, but so does environment.

1 As genetic similarities between subjects increase, so _____

2 As environments become more extreme, so _____

CHAPTER 6 Writing assignment

Choose one of the following topics as your chapter writing assignment.

1 In this chapter you read about the differences in intelligence between males and females and between the young and the old. To what extent did the research findings surprise you?

2 Which is more important in shaping an individual: heredity or environment? Do not confine your argument to the question of intelligence only; consider also, for example, the influence of these factors on an individual's belief system and personality.

3 Use examples of stories in history, literature, or movies to illustrate the notion that individuals can escape negative environmental influences and achieve their intellectual potentials.

Nonverbal Messages

In this unit we examine the ways in which human beings communicate nonverbally. In Chapter 7, we study the way in which we use our hands, face, and eyes to create meaningful nonverbal messages. In Chapter 8, we see that the ways we touch, the distances we create between ourselves and others, and the things we own may also speak louder than words and carry powerful unconscious messages.

PREVIEWING THE UNIT

Before reading a unit or chapter of a textbook, it is a good idea to preview the contents page and think about the topics that will be covered.

Read the contents page for Unit 4 and answer the following questions with a partner.

Chapter 7: Body language

1▸ In the first section of this chapter, "Universals of Nonverbal Communication," you will read that the total impact of a message comes from three factors: the words you choose, the physical movements you make, and the way you use your voice. Try to say the sentence, "It's time to go," in the following ways:

impatiently	in an uncertain manner	angrily
sadly	in a friendly manner	romantically

Discuss with your partner whether you can change the meaning of a message by the way you use your voice in your native language, too.

2▸ In the other three sections of Chapter 7, you will read about the different elements of body language. With your partner, make a list of the elements that you expect to read about. Decide which one you think is the single most powerful element of body language.

Chapter 8: The language of touch, space, and artifacts

1▸ In the first two sections of Chapter 8, you will read that the amount that people touch each other varies greatly from culture to culture. Is yours a "high-contact culture" (people touch a lot) or a "low-contact" one? Explain.

2▸ In "Space Communication," you will read about the different distances we usually keep between ourselves and others. Look at the diagram. Imagine that it represents the only free table and chairs in the school cafeteria. All the chairs at this table are empty except the one marked X. Where would you sit if the person seated at X is:

1 someone to whom you are attracted and would like to date, but to whom you have never spoken?

2 your boyfriend or girlfriend, with whom you are in love?

3 a favorite instructor whom you would like to get to know better?

4 an instructor who gave you an undeserved F in a course and whom you dislike intensely?

3▸ In the final section, "Artifactual Communication," you will read that the things we possess, such as our clothes, cars, and furniture, can communicate a lot about us. Describe (or show) three things that you own to your partner. Discuss what these things reveal about your personality and values.

UNIT CONTENTS

PREPARING TO READ

Previewing text headings

Before reading a text, it is a good idea to look at any headings that divide it. These can help you get an idea of the content, which makes the text easier to read.

1➤ Read the list of headings that divide this text into parts. With a partner, talk about the information that may be in each part.

1 Nonverbal Communication Occurs in a Context
2 Nonverbal Behaviors Are Usually Packaged
3 Nonverbal Behavior Always Communicates
4 Nonverbal Communication Is Governed by Rules
5 Nonverbal Communication Is Highly Believable

2➤ Now read the following extracts and with your partner guess which part of the text each one comes from. Write the number of the heading for that part in the blank.

____ *a* In the United States, direct eye contact signals openness and honesty. But in various countries of Latin America and among Native Americans, direct eye contact between, say, a teacher and a student, would be considered inappropriate.

____ *b* Pounding the fist on a table during a speech in support of a politician means something quite different from the same fist pounding in response to news of a friend's death.

____ *c* Albert Mehrabian (1976) argues that the total impact of a message is a function of the following formula: Total impact = .07 verbal + .38 vocal + .55 facial. This formula gives very little influence to verbal messages.

____ *d* Even small movements are extremely important in interpersonal relationships. We can often tell, for example, when two people genuinely like each other and when they are merely being polite.

____ *e* In fact, it is physically difficult to express an intense emotion with only one part of the body. Try to express an emotion with the face only. You will find that the rest of your body takes on the qualities of that emotion as well.

NOW READ

Now read the text "Universals of Nonverbal Communication." When you finish, check to see if your guesses were correct, and then turn to the tasks that begin on page 138.

1 *UNIVERSALS OF NONVERBAL COMMUNICATION*

Those characteristics that may be found in all forms of nonverbal communication are called "universals," and they provide a framework within which the specifics of nonverbal communication may be viewed.

NONVERBAL COMMUNICATION OCCURS IN A CONTEXT

Like verbal communication, nonverbal communication exists in a context, and that context determines to a large extent the meanings of any nonverbal behaviors. The same nonverbal behavior may have a totally different meaning when it occurs in another context. A wink of the eye to an attractive person on a bus means something completely different from a wink of an eye to signify a lie. Similarly, the meaning of a given bit of nonverbal behavior depends on the verbal behavior it accompanies or is close to in time. Pounding the fist on a table during a speech in support of a politician means something quite different from the same fist pounding in response to news of a friend's death. Of course, even if we know the context in detail, we still might not be able to decipher the meaning of the nonverbal behavior. In attempting to understand and analyze nonverbal communication, however, it is essential that full recognition be taken of the context.

NONVERBAL BEHAVIORS ARE USUALLY PACKAGED

Nonverbal behaviors, whether they involve the hands, the eyes, or the muscle tone of the body, usually occur in packages or *clusters* in which the various verbal and nonverbal behaviors reinforce each other, an occurrence referred to as *congruence*. We do not express fear with our eyes while the rest of our body relaxes as if sleeping; rather, the entire body expresses the emotion. We may, for the purposes of analysis, focus primarily on the eyes, the facial muscles, or the hand movement, but in everyday communication, these do not occur in isolation from other non-verbal behaviors. In fact, it is physically difficult to express an intense emotion with only one part of the body. Try to express an emotion with the face only. You will find that the rest of your body takes on the qualities of that emotion as well.

NONVERBAL BEHAVIOR ALWAYS COMMUNICATES

The observation that all behavior communicates is particularly important in regard to nonverbal communication. It is impossible not to behave; consequently, it is impossible not to communicate. Regardless of what one does or does not do, one's nonverbal behavior communicates something to someone (assuming that it occurs in an interactional setting).

Even small movements are extremely important in interpersonal relationships. We can often tell, for example, when two people genuinely like each other and when they are merely being polite. If we had to state how we know this, we would probably have considerable difficulty. These inferences, many of which are correct, are based primarily on these small nonverbal behaviors of the participants – the muscles around the eyes, the degree of eye contact, the way in which the individuals face each other, and so on. All nonverbal behavior, however small or transitory, is significant; all of it communicates.

NONVERBAL COMMUNICATION IS GOVERNED BY RULES

Nonverbal communication is rule-governed; it is regulated by a system of rules and norms that state what is and what is not appropriate, expected, and permissible in specific social situations. We learn both the ways to communicate nonverbally and the rules of appropriateness at the same time from observing the behaviors of the adult community. For example, we learn that touch is permissible under certain circumstances but not others, and we learn which type of touching is permissible and which is not; in short, we learn the rules governing touching behavior. We learn that women may touch each other in public; for example, they may hold hands, walk arm in arm, engage in prolonged hugging, and even dance together. We also learn that men may not do this, at least not without social criticism. Furthermore, we learn that there are certain parts of the body that may not be touched and certain parts that may. As a relationship changes, so do the rules for touching. As we become more intimate, the rules for touching become less restrictive.

In the United States, direct eye contact signals openness and honesty. But in various countries of Latin America and among Native Americans, direct eye contact between, say, a teacher and a student, would be con-

The rules of touching behavior do not usually allow men to come into close physical contact except in very specific situations, such as during sporting events.

sidered inappropriate, perhaps aggressive; appropriate student behavior would be to avoid eye contact with the teacher. From this simple example, it is easy to see how miscommunication can easily take place. To a teacher in the United States, avoidance of eye contact by a Latin American or Native American could easily be taken to mean guilt, disinterest, or disrespect, when in fact the child was following his or her own culturally established rules of eye contact. Like the nonverbal behaviors themselves, these rules are learned without conscious awareness. We learn them largely from observing others. The rules are brought to our attention only in formal discussions of nonverbal communication, such as this one, or when rules are violated and the violations are called to our attention – either directly by some tactless snob or indirectly through the examples of others. While linguists are attempting to formulate the rules for verbal messages, nonverbal researchers are attempting to formulate the rules for nonverbal messages – rules that native communicators know and use every day, but cannot necessarily verbalize.

NONVERBAL BEHAVIOR IS HIGHLY BELIEVABLE

For some reasons, not all of which are clear to researchers, we are quick to believe nonverbal behaviors even when these behaviors contradict verbal messages. Nonverbal theorist Dale Leathers (1990), for example, reports on research demonstrating that, compared to verbal cues, nonverbal cues are four times as effective in their impact on interpersonal impressions and ten times more important in expressing confidence. From a different perspective, Albert Mehrabian (1976) argues that the total impact of a message is a function of the following formula:

The eye contact of these two people is governed by rules outside their conscious awareness.

$$\text{Total impact} = .07 \text{ verbal} + .38 \text{ vocal} + .55 \text{ facial}$$

This formula gives very little influence to verbal messages. Only one third of the impact is vocal (that is, **paralanguage** elements such as rate, pitch, and rhythm) and over one half of the message is communicated by the face. The formula, developed by Mehrabian and his colleagues from their studies on the emotional impact of messages, is not applicable to all messages; it is applicable only to the expression of feelings. Although it is interesting to speculate on what percentage of message impact is due to nonverbal elements in other kinds of messages, there is no valid and reliable answer at this time.

paralanguage
the vocal (but nonverbal) dimension of speech that can convey information, especially about a speaker's attitude

   Why we believe the nonverbal message over the verbal message is not clear. It may be that we feel verbal messages are easier to fake. Thus, when there is a contradiction, we distrust the verbal and accept the nonverbal. Or it may be that the nonverbal messages function below the level of conscious awareness. We learned them without being aware of such learning, and we perceive them without conscious awareness. Consequently, when such a conflict arises, we somehow get this "feeling" from the nonverbal messages. Since we cannot isolate its source, we assume that it is somehow correct.

AFTER YOU READ

Task 1 Analyzing the organization of a text

> When a text is divided into parts (usually with headings), each part focuses on a different aspect of the overall topic. In each part there will be a main idea, examples to support that idea, and often some additional commentary or remarks about the main idea.

1▶ Skim through each part of the text and underline the sentence or sentences that contain the main idea.

2▶ Skim through each part again. Identify items of supporting evidence or examples for the main idea by inserting a number in front of each one and drawing a slash (/) to indicate where the example or support ends. In the blank, write in the number of pieces of support for the main idea in each part of the text.

_____ Nonverbal Communication Occurs in a Context
_____ Nonverbal Behaviors Are Usually Packaged
_____ Nonverbal Behavior Always Communicates
_____ Nonverbal Communication Is Governed by Rules
_____ Nonverbal Communication Is Highly Believable

3▶ You have identified the main ideas and the evidence to support those ideas. What remains may be called commentary. Read through the commentary in each part and decide if the following statements are true (T) or false (F).

_____ *1* If we know the full context for a piece of nonverbal behavior, we can always understand its meaning.
_____ *2* It is not easy to express an emotion with just one part of your body; the rest of the body will move automatically.
_____ *3* Tiny body movements do not play a significant part in communicating a message.
_____ *4* We are usually taught the rules for appropriate nonverbal behavior in school.
_____ *5* Mehrabian's formula is not applicable to all verbal messages, only to those expressing emotion.

Task 2 Language focus: Transitional expressions

> Transitional expressions are phrases that show the relationship between different parts of a text. Like signposts on the road, they show where you are going and where you have come from. They can show, for example, that you are about to read an explanation, a cause, an additional point, etc. Being aware of them can help you improve your comprehension of a text.

In this text, there are many transitional expressions. Some of these expressions, shown in italics, are given in context in list A. In each example, the transitional expression shows the relationship between two ideas or pieces of information: the first idea is highlighted; the second idea is represented by a blank.

Decide what kind of information you would expect to find in the blank. Choose your answer from list B and write the correct letter in the blank. The first one has been done for you.

A Transitional expressions in context

1 A wink of the eye to an attractive person on a bus means . . . *Similarly*, ___f___ .

2 . . . *even if* we know the context in detail, we *still* _____.

3 We do not express fear with our eyes . . . , *rather* the entire body _____.

4 . . . these movements do not occur in isolation. . . . *In fact*, _____.

5 We learn that touch is permissible under certain circumstances; . . . *in short*, _____.

6 We learn that women may touch each other in public; . . . *Furthermore*, we learn _____.

7 *Like* the nonverbal behaviors themselves, these rules _____.

8 . . . only in formal discussions of nonverbal communication, *such as* _____.

9 Only one third of the impact is vocal, *that is* _____.

10 It may be that we feel verbal messages are easier to fake. *Thus*, _____.

B The blank should contain:

a an example
b an expanded explanation or clarification
c a summary of what has just been stated
d a contrasting fact or idea
e a fact that is different from what one might expect
f a fact or idea similar to the one just stated
g a consequence or effect of what has just been stated
h an idea that provides additional support

Task 3 Writing: Using transitional expressions

It is important to practice using transitional expressions in your writing. Using them correctly will make your writing clearer, easier to read, and more convincing.

Complete the sentences in the list using concepts found in this text.

1 It is important to know the context of any nonverbal behavior. For example, you may assume that someone with tears in his or her eyes is unhappy. In fact, . . .

2 Nonverbal communication is usually "packaged," that is, . . .

3 Nonverbal communication always communicates. Even if we try to control . . .

4 Nonverbal behavior is governed by rules. These rules are not consciously taught to us by our parents or teachers, rather . . .

PREPARING TO READ

Thinking about the topic

In this text you are going to read about a classification of gestures into five different categories:

emblems	affect displays	regulators
illustrators	adaptors	

The five pairs of situations in the table illustrate the five different kinds of gestures. After you read the text, you will be asked to name the kind of gesture used for each pair. For now, read each situation and show your classmates what gesture you might make in each one.

What would you do . . .	Category of gesture
1 a to show someone that you are very angry with him?	
b to show someone that you think what she just said was absolutely amazing?	
2 a to show someone that you are listening very carefully to what he is saying to you?	
b to show someone that you have finished speaking and now you want her to respond in some way?	
3 a to show someone that what he just did was perfect, just great?	
b to show someone that you think another person, perhaps across the room, is absolutely crazy?	
4 a if you were sitting alone and you had an itch on your chin?	
b if your lips were dry and you wanted to moisten them (make them wet)?	
5 a if you were telling someone that you caught a big fish?	
b if you were explaining to someone how you caught a ball?	

NOW READ

Now read the text "Gestural Communication." When you finish, write in the category of gesture that would be used for each pair of situations listed above. Then turn to the tasks that begin on page 144.

2 GESTURAL COMMUNICATION

In dealing with nonverbal body gestures or movements (sometimes called **kinesics**), a classification offered by Paul Ekman and Wallace V. Friesen (1969) seems the most useful. These researchers distinguish five classes of nonverbal movements based on the origins, functions, and coding of the behavior: emblems, illustrators, affect displays, regulators, and adaptors.

kinesics
the study of human body movements and their conscious and unconscious meanings

EMBLEMS

Emblems are nonverbal behaviors that translate words or phrases rather directly. Emblems include, for example, the nonverbal signs for OK, peace, come here, go away, who me?, be quiet, I'm warning you, I'm tired, and it's cold. Emblems are nonverbal substitutes for specific verbal words or phrases and are probably learned in essentially the same way as are specific words and phrases, without conscious awareness or explicit teaching and largely through imitation. Although emblems seem rather natural to us and almost inherently meaningful, they are as arbitrary as any word in any language. Consequently, our present culture's emblems are not necessarily the same as our culture's emblems of 300 years ago or the same as the emblems of other cultures. For example, the OK sign may mean "nothing" or "zero" in France, "money" in Japan, and something sexual in certain Latin American cultures. Just as the English language is spreading throughout the world, so too is English nonverbal language. The meaning of the thumb and index finger forming a circle meaning "OK" is spreading just as fast as, for example, English technical and scientific terms.

Emblems are often used to supplement the verbal message or as a kind of reinforcement. At times they are used in place of verbalization, for example, when there is a considerable distance between the individuals and shouting would be inappropriate or when we wish to communicate something behind someone's back.

This gesture may mean different things in different cultures. Its American meaning is "Everything is OK."

ILLUSTRATORS

Illustrators are nonverbal behaviors that accompany and literally illustrate the verbal messages. Illustrators make our communications more vivid and more forceful and help to maintain the attention of the listener. They also help to clarify and make more intense our verbal messages. In saying, "Let's go up," for example, there will be movements of the head and perhaps hands going in an upward direction. In describing a circle or a square, you are more than likely going to make circular or square movements with your hands.

We are aware of illustrators only part of the time; at times they may have to be brought to our attention and our awareness. Illustrators seem more natural and less arbitrary than emblems. They are partly a function

Illustrators are gestures that make a verbal message more vivid by producing a picture in the air.

of learning and partly innate. Illustrators are more universal; they are more common throughout the world and throughout time than emblems.

AFFECT DISPLAYS

Affect displays are the movements of the facial area that convey emotional meaning – the facial expressions that show anger and fear, happiness and surprise, eagerness and fatigue. They are the facial expressions that "give us away" when we try to hide how we are really feeling, and that lead people to say, "You look angry. What's wrong?" We can, however, also consciously control affect displays, as actors do when they play a role. Affect displays are more independent of verbal messages than illustrators and less under conscious control than either emblems or illustrators.

Affect displays may be unintentional, as when they give us away, but they may also be intentional. We may want to show anger or love or hate or surprise, and, for the most part, we do a creditable job.

REGULATORS

Regulators are nonverbal behaviors that "regulate" (monitor, maintain, or control) the speaking of another individual. When we listen to another, we are not passive; we nod our heads, purse our lips, adjust our eye focus, and make various paralinguistic sounds such as "mm-mm" or "tsk." Regulators are clearly culture-bound and are not universal.

Regulators in effect convey to speakers what we expect or want them to do as they are talking – "Keep going," "What else happened?," "I don't believe that," "Speed up," "Slow down," and any number of other directions. Speakers often receive these nonverbal behaviors without being consciously aware of them. Depending on their degree of sensitivity, they modify their speaking behavior in line with the directions supplied by the regulators. Regulators would also include such gross movements as turning one's head or leaning forward in one's chair.

ADAPTORS

Adaptors are nonverbal behaviors designed to satisfy some need. Sometimes the need is physical, as when we scratch to satisfy an itch or when we push our hair out of our eyes. Sometimes the need is psychological, as when we bite our lip when anxious. Sometimes adaptors are directed at increasing comfort, as when we moisten dry lips. When these adaptors occur in private, they occur in their entirety. We scratch our head until the itch is gone; we pick our nose until we're satisfied. But in public these adaptors usually occur in abbreviated form. For example, when people are watching us, we might put our fingers to our head and move them around a bit but probably not scratch with the same vigor as when in private. Because publicly emitted adaptors usually occur in abbreviated form, it is often difficult for an observer to tell what this partial behavior was intended to accomplish. For example, observing someone's finger on one's head, we cannot be certain for what this behavior was intended.

Adaptors usually occur without conscious awareness; they are unintentional movements that usually go unnoticed. Generally, researchers report, adaptors are signs of negative feelings. For example, we emit more adaptors when we feel hostile than when we feel friendly. Further, as anxiety and uneasiness increase, so does the frequency of adaptors.

Increased use of adaptors is often a sign of anxiety or uneasiness.

AFTER YOU READ

Task 1 Highlighting

> **R**emember, when you highlight a text, it is a good idea to use several different colors systematically. For example, use one color for definitions of key terms and a second color for examples of these terms.

1► Find definitions of the following key terms in this text and highlight them.

emblems	affect displays	regulators
illustrators	adaptors	

2► Find examples of each of the five gesture types and highlight them in a different color.

3► Following the definitions and examples of each gesture type, the author adds important observations or commentary about each one. Find this commentary and highlight it in a third color. For example, in the part of the text on "emblems," you would highlight the following:

> Emblems . . . probably learned . . . without conscious awareness or explicit teaching and largely through imitation.

> Consequently, our present culture's emblems are not necessarily the same as our culture's emblems of 300 years ago or the same as the emblems of other cultures.

> Just as the English language is spreading throughout the world, so too is English nonverbal language.

> Emblems are often used to supplement the verbal message. . . . At times they are used in place of verbalization. . . .

4► Compare answers with a partner and see if you have highlighted the same definitions, examples, and commentary.

Task 2 Note-taking practice

> **N**otes should be brief, complete, and easy to read. Although there are useful guidelines for how to take effective notes (see page 101 for a list), ultimately you may want to develop a system of note-taking that works for you.

1► Look at how one student took notes for the part of the text under the heading, "Emblems." Then use your own note-taking system to take notes on another part of the text.

```
Emblems

Def – nonverb. behaviors that translate words or phrases
Ex – thumb + forefing. = OK

1   prob. learned unconsciously

2   embs diff in diff times + cults

    Ex – OK sign  =  O in France
                     money in Japan
                     sex in Lat Am.

3   Engl. embs spreading in world, e.g., OK sign

4   embs often supplement verb. messg.
```

2► Work with a partner. Using only your notes, give your partner an oral summary of the part of the text you took notes on.

Task 3 Thinking critically about the text

> Testing a key concept or hypothesis in a text can help you think critically about what you have read and help you develop a greater understanding of the concept.

1► According to this text, not all cultures use the same emblem gestures. Test this idea by asking people from different cultures to show you what gestures they would make in order to communicate the following:

I am sleepy.	Please forgive me.
I am broke.	Good luck.
I have no idea.	Come here.
I am thinking.	Good-bye.
I am hungry.	You are late.

2► Think of an emblem gesture used in your country that you think may have a different meaning in another country. Make the gesture and ask classmates who come from a different country what it means.

3► Discuss whether you see any evidence that American nonverbal language is spreading throughout the world.

PREPARING TO READ

Conducting an experiment

> **C**onducting an experiment that tests a key concept or hypothesis in a text will make it easier to understand the concept. It will also help you recall the details of the text and the nature of the issues under discussion later on.

According to a key hypothesis presented in this text, facial expressions are largely universal. If this is so, all the students in your class should choose the same answers in the following activities, regardless of their age, sex, or cultural background.

1➤ Find the face that best expresses each emotion and write the letter of that face in the blank. Compare answers with your classmates.

_____ happiness   _____ anger   _____ fear
_____ sadness   _____ disgust   _____ interest

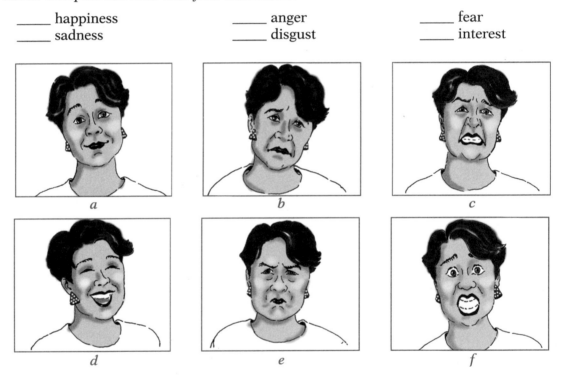

a   b   c

d   e   f

2➤ Work with a partner. Choose one of the emotions listed above and make a facial expression to show that emotion. See if your partner can guess the emotion from your expression.

NOW READ

Now read the text "Facial Communication." When you finish, turn to the tasks that begin on page 149.

3 FACIAL COMMUNICATION

Throughout our interpersonal interactions, our faces communicate, especially our emotions. Paul Ekman, Wallace V. Friesen, and Phoebe Ellsworth (1972) claim that facial messages may communicate at least the following eight emotions: happiness, surprise, fear, anger, sadness, disgust, contempt, and interest. Dale Leathers (1990) has proposed that in addition to these eight, facial movements may also communicate bewilderment and determination.

Try to communicate surprise using only facial movements. Do this in front of a mirror and attempt to describe in as much detail as possible the specific movements of the face that make up surprise. If you signal surprise like most people, you probably employ raised and curved eyebrows, long horizontal forehead wrinkles, wide-open eyes, a dropped-open mouth, and lips parted with no tension. Even if there were differences – and clearly there would be from one person to another – you could probably recognize the movements listed here as indicative of surprise. In **FAST** (facial affect scoring technique), the face is broken up into three main parts: eyebrows and forehead, eyes and eyelids, and the lower face from the bridge of the nose down (Ekman, Friesen, and Tomkins, 1971). Judges then try to identify various emotions by observing the different parts of the face and writing descriptions similar to the one just given for surprise. In this way we can study more effectively just how the face communicates the various emotions.

> **FAST**
> facial affect scoring technique – a system devised to help researchers identify the facial expressions that typically accompany certain emotions

COMMUNICATION ACCURACY

The accuracy with which people express emotions facially and the accuracy with which receivers decode the expressions have been the objects of considerable research. One problem confronting this research is that it is difficult to separate the ability of the encoder from the ability of the decoder. Thus a person may be quite adept at communicating emotions, but the receiver may prove to be insensitive. On the other hand, the receiver may be quite good at deciphering emotions, but the sender may be inept. And, of course, there are tremendous differences from one person to another and with the same person at different times.

A second problem is that accuracy seems to vary with the method of the research. In some cases still photographs are used and people are asked to judge the emotions the people are experiencing. Some research uses live models or actors and actresses who have been trained to communicate the different emotions. Still others use more spontaneous methods. For example, an individual judge views a person who is herself or himself viewing and reacting to a film. The judge, without seeing the film, has to decode the emotion the viewer is experiencing. As can be appreciated, each method yields somewhat different results. Accuracy also varies with emotions themselves. Some emotions are easier to communicate and decode than others. Ekman, Friesen, and Carlsmith (1972) report, for example, that happiness is judged with an accuracy ranging

There is evidence to suggest that some facial expressions, such as smiling, are universal; that is, they mean the same thing in all cultures.

from 55 to 100 percent, surprise from 38 to 86 percent, and sadness from 19 to 88 percent. All this is not to say that the results of these studies are of no value; it is merely to inject a note of caution in dealing with "conclusions" about facial communication.

UNIVERSAL OR RELATIVE?

It appears from cross-cultural research that facial expressions have a somewhat universal nature. For example, people in Borneo and New Guinea who have had little contact with Western cultures were able to match accurately emotions with pictures of facial expressions of Westerners. Further, their own facial expressions, posed to communicate different emotions, were accurately decoded by Americans. Similarly, in studies conducted with children who were born blind and who therefore could not see how others facially expressed the various emotions, the children seem to use the same facial expressions as their sighted peers. Studies such as these point to a universality among facial gestures. The wide variations in facial communication that we do observe in different cultures seem to reflect what is permissible and not permissible to communicate, rather than a difference in the way in which emotions are expressed facially (Matsumoto, 1991). For example, in some cultures it is permissible openly and publicly to show contempt or disgust, but in others people are taught to hide such emotions in public and to display them only in private.

AFTER YOU READ

Task 1 Turning written text into a graphic

> **W**hen you read, you can sometimes make the meaning clearer to yourself by creating a graphic.

1▶ Draw the following details onto the face in the figure.

- raised and curved eyebrows
- long horizontal wrinkles on the forehead
- wide-open eyes
- a dropped-open mouth

2▶ Now draw two lines across the face to show the three parts of the face used in FAST.

3▶ Reread the fourth paragraph in "Facial Communication." Find the description of the experiment in which a judge views a person viewing a film. Draw a small diagram showing the set-up for the experiment.

Task 2 Building vocabulary: Guessing meaning from context

> **I**t is often possible to get a general idea of the meaning of a word or phrase by looking at its context.

Read these passages from the text and use the context to work out what the words in bold probably mean.

> One problem confronting this research is that it is difficult to separate the ability of the **encoder** from the ability of the **decoder**. Thus a person may be quite **adept** at communicating emotions, but the receiver may prove to be insensitive. On the other hand, the receiver may be quite good at **deciphering** emotions, but the sender may be **inept**.

encoder _____

decoder _____

adept _____

deciphering _____

inept _____

In some cases **still photographs** are used and people are asked to judge the emotions the people are experiencing. Some research uses **live models** or actors and actresses who have been trained to communicate the different emotions. Still others use more **spontaneous methods**. For example, an individual judge views a person who is herself or himself viewing and reacting to a film. The judge, without seeing the film, has to decode the emotion the viewer is experiencing.

still photographs _____

live models _____

spontaneous methods _____

Similarly, in studies **conducted** with children who were **born blind** and who therefore could not see how others facially expressed the various emotions, the children seem to use the same facial expressions as their **sighted peers**.

conducted _____

born blind _____

sighted peers _____

Task 3 Test-taking: Writing short answers to test questions

Since a perfect answer to even a short-answer test question will usually include several pieces of information, be sure to read each question carefully and think about everything that should be included in a correct answer. The more complete your answer, the more points your teacher will give.

1➤ Read the following three questions on this text and the answers given by one student. If a perfect answer gets 10 points, how many points would you give for each of these answers?

1 What is FAST?

FAST is a method of dividing the face into parts so that when someone expresses an emotion you can describe each part and thus have a description of the facial expression for that emotion.

score: _____ points

2   Name three methods used by researchers to judge an individual's ability to decode emotions.

> *There are several ways of judging an individual's ability to decode an emotion. One way is to have them look at photographs of people with different emotions and ask them to say what emotion the person is feeling. Another way is to ask a person to express a particular emotion on his or her face.*

score: _____ points

3   What evidence is there that facial expressions are universal?

> *When people in Borneo are asked to express a particular emotion, they make the same facial expressions as people asked to do the same thing in the United States. Also, children who are born blind have the same facial expressions as people who can see.*

score: _____ points

2▶ Compare your scores in a small group. Explain why you gave each score. For any answer which you decided not to give a perfect score, describe how you think the answer could be improved.

Follow-up: Writing a short answer

Write your own answer to one of the questions above. Close your book and give yourself a time limit. When you have finished writing, give your answer to another student to score it (a perfect answer gets 10 points). After you score each other's questions, explain why you gave the score that you did.

PREPARING TO READ

Building vocabulary: Collocations

> Remember, do not just learn single new words. Be aware of how words occur in phrases and collocations.

1➤ The following collocations of "eye contact" occur in the text:

to [make / hold / maintain / return / break / avoid] eye contact

Put these verbs (in their correct grammatical forms) into the following story. Use each verb once.

I walked into the party and saw the most attractive man I have ever seen in my whole life. I desperately wanted to meet him, so I tried to _____ eye contact. I could see that he noticed me looking at him, but he just refused to _____ my eye contact. He just kept _____ having any eye contact with me. Then I noticed that he _____ my eye contact for a second or two before _____ it. I went up to the bar where he was standing and stood next to him, and we both looked at each other and _____ eye contact for a full three seconds. "Do I know you?" he asked. My heart almost stopped beating. He continued, "I'm afraid I've lost my glasses and I can't see a thing."

2➤ The following verbal expressions, taken from the text and listed in the left-hand column below, also describe "ways of looking." Match each expression on the left with an equivalent expression on the right.

_____ *1* lock eyes with someone   *a* avoid looking at someone

_____ *2* gaze   *b* look someone over from head to toe

_____ *3* look very intently   *c* get someone's attention

_____ *4* sweep one's eyes over someone   *d* watch (for example, a television show)

_____ *5* catch someone's eye   *e* look casually, without great intensity

_____ *6* avert one's glance   *f* stare

_____ *7* view   *g* make eye contact with someone and hold it

Speed reading

Use this text as an opportunity to practice your speed-reading skills. Before you start, review the guidelines for faster reading on page 36 in Chapter 2.

NOW READ

Now read the text "Eye Communication." Time yourself. When you finish, make a note of how long it took you to read the text. Then turn to the tasks that begin on page 155.

4 EYE COMMUNICATION

From the observations of poets to the scientific observations of contemporary researchers, the eyes are regarded as the most important nonverbal message system.

EYE CONTACT FUNCTIONS

Mark Knapp (1978), as well as various other researchers, notes four major functions of eye communication.

To monitor feedback In talking with someone, we look at the person intently, as if to say, "Well, what do you think?" or "React to what I've just said." Also, we look at speakers to let them know that we are listening. In studies conducted on gazing behavior and summarized by Knapp and Hall (1992), it has been found that listeners gaze at speakers more than speakers gaze at listeners. The percentage of interaction time spent gazing while listening, for example, has been observed in two studies to be 62 percent and 75 percent, while the percentage of time spent gazing while talking has been observed to be 38 percent and 41 percent. When these percentages are reversed – when a speaker gazes at the listener for longer than "normal" periods or when a listener gazes at the speaker for shorter than "normal" periods – the conversational interaction becomes awkward and uncomfortable. You may wish to try this with a friend; even with mutual awareness, you will note the discomfort caused by this seemingly minor communication change.

To signal a conversational turn A second and related function is to inform the other person that the channel of communication is open and that she or he should now speak. The clearest example of this is seen in the college classroom, where the instructor asks a question and then locks eyes with a student. Without any verbal message, it is assumed that the student should answer the question.

To signal the nature of the relationship A third function is to signal the nature of the relationship between two people, for example, one of positive or negative regard. When we like someone, we increase our eye contact. Nonverbal researcher Michael Argyle (1988), for example, notes that when eye contact goes beyond 60 percent, the individuals are probably more interested in each other than in the verbal messages being exchanged. Another relational message that eye contact communicates is the individual's willingness to pursue the development of a relationship. When direct eye contact is made, held for a few moments, and when each person's eyes sweep over the other's body and then return to direct eye contact, we may reasonably predict (especially if accompanied by a smile) that each would willingly pursue a get-together. If, on the other hand, after direct eye contact is made, it is broken quickly and not returned, we may reasonably predict that this is not a relationship that will blossom very quickly.

What does this couple's eye contact tell you about their feelings toward each other?

To compensate for physical distance   Eye movements are often used to compensate for increased physical distance. By making eye contact, we overcome psychologically the physical distance between us. When we catch someone's eye at a party, for example, we become psychologically close even though we may be separated by considerable physical distance.

EYE AVOIDANCE FUNCTIONS

The eyes, observed sociologist Erving Goffman in "Interaction Ritual" (1967) are "great intruders." When we avoid eye contact or avert our glance, we enable others to maintain their privacy. We frequently do this when a couple argues, say in the street or on a bus. We turn our eyes away (though our ears may be wide open) as if to say, "We don't mean to intrude; we respect your privacy." Goffman refers to this behavior as *civil inattention.*

Eye avoidance can signal disinterest in a person, a conversation, or some visual stimulus. At times, like the ostrich, we hide our eyes in an attempt to cut off unpleasant stimuli. Notice, for example, how quickly people close their eyes in the face of some extreme unpleasantness. Interestingly enough, even if the unpleasantness is auditory, we tend to shut it out by closing our eyes. Sometimes we close our eyes to block out visual stimuli and thus heighten our other senses; we often listen to music with our eyes closed. Lovers often close their eyes while kissing, and many prefer to make love in a dark or dimly lit room.

PUPIL DILATION

In addition to eye movements, considerable research has been done on pupil dilation. In the fifteenth and sixteenth centuries in Italy, women used to put drops of belladonna (which literally means "beautiful woman") into their eyes to enlarge the pupils so that they would look more attractive. Contemporary research seems to support the intuitive logic of these women; dilated pupils are in fact judged to be more attractive than constricted pupils (Hess, 1975; Marshall, 1983).

In one study, photographs of women were retouched (Hess, 1975). On one set the pupils were enlarged, and in another they were made smaller. Men were then shown the photographs and asked to judge the women's personalities. The photos of women with small pupils drew responses such as cold, hard, and selfish; those with dilated pupils drew responses such as feminine and soft. The male observers, however, could not verbalize the reasons for the different perceptions. Pupil dilation and reactions to changes in the pupil size of others both seem to function below our level of awareness.

Pupil size is also indicative of one's interest and level of emotional arousal. One's pupils enlarge when one is interested in something or when one is emotionally aroused. Perhaps we judge dilated pupils as more attractive because we judge the individual's dilated pupils to be indicative of an interest in us.

You may feel differently about the woman in the top photograph than you do about the woman in the bottom one.

AFTER YOU READ

Time it took you to read the text: _____ (to the nearest tenth of a minute, for example, 3.4 minutes).

Task 1 Reading for detail

Test your understanding of the text by answering these multiple-choice reading comprehension questions without looking back at the text. Choose the best answer from the choices listed.

1 According to the text, the eyes are _____ important nonverbal message givers.

   a the most

   b one of the most

   c the least

2 How many major functions of eye contact does Mark Knapp describe?

   a three

   b four

   c five

3 Who looks at whom more during an interaction?

   a The speaker looks more at the listener.

   b The listener looks more at the speaker.

   c The listener and speaker both look at each other about the same amount.

4 One of the functions of eye contact, as seen in the example of when an instructor may look at a student, is _____.

   a to show disapproval

   b to show it is the listener's turn to speak

   c to show that you are pleased with someone

5 If you see someone at a party whom you would like to get to know better, and this person makes eye contact with you and then breaks it very quickly, this is _____.

   a a sign that the person is probably very shy but would like to get to know you

   b a sign that the person is flirting with you

   c a sign that the person is probably not interested in getting to know you

6 We tend to make eye contact more than normal with someone when _____.

   a we are physically a little distant from them

   b we do not particularly like them

   c we are standing very close to them

7 One reason for avoiding eye contact is so that _____.

   a people will not be able to see what we are thinking

   b we will be able to listen better to someone's private conversation

   c we may give someone the sense that we are respecting their privacy

8 We may close our eyes to _____.

    a block some unpleasant sensation

    b be even more aware of a pleasant sensation

    c do either of the above

9 If a photograph of a woman is changed to make her pupils look larger, men will tend to judge the woman as _____.

    a being more attractive

    b having a colder personality

    c appearing more selfish

10 What happens to the pupils of the eyes when someone is emotionally aroused?

    a They become smaller.

    b They become larger.

    c They appear to become larger but, in fact, they stay the same size.

Follow-up: How well did you read?

1➤ Reread the text and check your answers to the reading comprehension questions.

2➤ Fill in the box to calculate your reading speed in words per minute (wpm) and your percent correct on the reading comprehension questions. A good goal would be to read at about 250 wpm with an accuracy of 70 percent.

a time to read	_____
b number of words	_____ 937 _____
c wpm (*b/a*)	_____
d number correct	_____
e percent correct (*d* x 10)	_____

Task 2 Dramatizing the text

> **R**ole-playing can breathe life into an abstract concept, such as eye contact norms, and make it seem very real and concrete.

You have read that there is an acceptable, normal length for eye contact between listener and speaker during an interaction. What happens when you break these norms? Work with a partner and find out. Take turns at being either a listener or a speaker. Try each of the different speaker/listener roles in the list that follows and then discuss how you felt in each situation. (Speakers should talk about any general topic: their family, interests, habits, last weekend, and so on.)

1	*Listener:*	Look at speaker without breaking eye contact at any time.
	Speaker:	Look at listener without breaking eye contact.
2	*Listener:*	Do not make eye contact with speaker at any time.
	Speaker:	Do not make eye contact with speaker.
3	*Listener:*	Do not make eye contact with speaker at any time.
	Speaker:	Look at listener as you normally would, sometimes making and sometimes breaking eye contact.
4	*Listener:*	Look at listener as you normally would, sometimes making and sometimes breaking eye contact.
	Speaker:	Do not make eye contact with listener at any time.

Task 3 Writing a summary

> **W**riting a summary is a useful way to check whether you have understood the main ideas of a text. It is also a good way to prepare for a test.

Read through the text again and then write a one-paragraph summary of either:

a the part about eye contact functions, or
b the part about pupil dilation.

Remember to include only the most important information.

CHAPTER 7 Writing assignment

Choose one of the following topics as your chapter writing assignment.

1 What evidence is there to suggest that body language is universal? Consider evidence from all sections of the chapter.

2 Compare body language in your culture with that of any other culture you are familiar with. Refer to the elements of gesture, facial expressions, and eye contact.

3 Evaluate how the information in the chapter might affect the way in which you behave in the future. In particular, how might your behavior change if you are currently living in, or planning soon to be living in, another culture?

PREPARING TO READ

Thinking about the topic

Work with a partner and brainstorm a list of as many different situations as you can in which it is permissible or acceptable for one person to touch another person in your culture. Note which part of the body is used to make the touch, on which part of the body the touch may occur, and who the toucher and touched might be. For example:

A stranger might tap (touch lightly with his or her fingers) another stranger on the shoulder in order to get the other's attention.

The following verbs that describe different ways of touching may help give you some ideas.

caress	poke	slap	nudge
hug	kiss	smack	tickle
prod	pat	punch	

Skimming for main ideas

You can get a general idea of a text before you read it just by skimming, or reading the headings and the first couple of lines of each paragraph.

Skim through the text, reading no more than the first two lines of each paragraph. As you read, answer the following questions.

Paragraph 1	What is a technical term for touch communication?
Paragraph 3	In "positive affect" touching, what is the usual relationship between those who are touching?
Paragraph 4	Can "playful" touching sometimes be aggressive?
Paragraphs 5 and 6	What can a "control" touch direct?
Paragraph 7	Ritual touching most typically occurs in which situations?
Paragraph 8	What is an example of a "task-related" touch?

NOW READ

Now read the text "The Meanings of Touch." As you read, check to see if you answered the questions above correctly. When you finish reading, turn to the tasks on page 161.

CHAPTER 8

The Language of Touch, Space, and Artifacts

---

1   THE MEANINGS OF TOUCH

Touch communication, also referred to as **haptics**, is perhaps the most [1]
primitive form of communication. Developmentally, touch is probably
the first sense to be used; even in the womb the child is stimulated by
touch. Soon after birth the child is caressed, patted, and stroked. In turn,
the child explores its world through touch. In a very short time, the child
learns to communicate a wide variety of meanings through touch.

> **haptics**
> the study of human touch
> behavior

Five of the major meanings of touch, identified in an extensive study [2]
by Stanley Jones and Elaine Yarborough (1985), are considered here.

POSITIVE AFFECT

Touch may communicate positive emotions. This touching occurs main- [3]
ly between intimates or others who have a relatively close relationship.
"Touch is such a powerful signaling system," notes Desmond Morris
(1974), "and it's so closely related to emotional feelings we have for one
another that in casual encounters it's kept to a minimum. When the relationship develops, the touching follows along with it." Among the most
important of these positive emotions are support, which indicates nur-
turing, reassurance, or protection; appreciation, which expresses grati-
tude; inclusion, which suggests psychological closeness; sexual interest
or intent; and affection, which expresses a generalized positive regard for
the other person.

PLAYFULNESS

4 Touch often communicates our intention to play, either affectionately or aggressively. When affection or aggression is communicated in a playful manner, the playfulness de-emphasizes the emotion and tells the other person that it is not to be taken seriously. Playful touches serve to lighten an interaction.

CONTROL

5 Touch may also serve to direct the behaviors, attitudes, or feelings of the other person. Such control may communicate a number of messages. In compliance, for example, we touch the other person to communicate "move over," "hurry," "stay here," and "do it." In attention-getting, we touch the person to gain his or her attention, as if to say "look at me" or "look over here."

6 Touching to control may also communicate dominance. Consider, as Nancy Henley suggests in her *Body Politics* (1977), who would touch whom – say, by putting an arm on the other person's shoulder or by putting a hand on the other person's back – in the following dyads: teacher and student, doctor and patient, master and servant, manager and worker, minister and parishioner, police officer and accused, business person and secretary. Most people brought up in our culture would say the first-named person in each dyad would be more likely to touch the second-named person than the other way around. In other words, it is the higher status person who is permitted to touch the lower status person.

RITUAL

7 Ritualistic touching centers on greetings and departures. Shaking hands to say "hello" or "good-bye" is perhaps the clearest example of ritualistic touching, but we might also hug, kiss, or put our arm around another's shoulder in meeting someone or in anticipating the person's departure.

TASK-RELATEDNESS

8 Task-related touching is associated with the performance of some function; this ranges from removing a speck of dust from another person's face to helping someone out of a car or checking someone's forehead for a fever.

In most cultures, people who do not know each other will rarely touch, except in some acceptable ritual such as a greeting.

AFTER YOU READ

Task 1 Reading for detail

1► Match each category of touch to one of the five situations described.

   a Positive Affect
   b Playfulness
   c Control
   d Ritual
   e Task-relatedness

     _____ *1* A teacher holds a student's arm and leads her down the hall to see the principal.
     _____ *2* A husband and wife walk arm in arm down the street.
     _____ *3* Two college students give each other a "high five" when they meet on campus.
     _____ *4* One child tickles his friend during recess on the playground.
     _____ *5* As a sales assistant gives you your change, your two hands touch for a split second.

2► Think of your own example for each of the five categories of touch.

Task 2 Writing

1► In the picture on page 160, you see two people touching as they greet each other. Discuss with a partner how people greet each other in your country. Note whether the manner of greeting depends on the sex and age of the people greeting, and/or how well they know each other.

2► Organize your ideas into a short piece of writing.

PREPARING TO READ

Thinking about the topic

1 ▶ Think about whether it would feel strange to you if you were touched casually on the following parts of your body by a same-sex friend or an opposite-sex friend. Circle your answer. Use the following scale: 1= very strange, I wouldn't like it at all; 2 = a little strange, I'd feel it was unusual; 3 = not strange at all, I would hardly notice it.

Same-sex friend				Opposite-sex friend		
1	2	3	on the top of the head	1	2	3
1	2	3	on the face	1	2	3
1	2	3	on the shoulder	1	2	3
1	2	3	on the arms	1	2	3
1	2	3	on the hand	1	2	3
1	2	3	on the bottom	1	2	3
1	2	3	on the thigh	1	2	3
1	2	3	on the knee	1	2	3
1	2	3	on the foot	1	2	3

2 ▶ If possible, compare your answers with:

- someone of the same sex, and from the same cultural background
- someone of the same sex, but from a different cultural background
- someone of the opposite sex, and from the same cultural background
- someone of the opposite sex, but from a different cultural background

In the appropriate square in the grid below, depending on the sex and culture of each partner, circle either *similar* or *different* to indicate whether your answers and your partner's answers were similar or different.

	same sex	*opposite sex*
same culture	similar/different	similar/different
different culture	similar/different	similar/different

NOW READ

Now read the text "Gender and Cultural Differences in Touching." When you finish, turn to the tasks that begin on page 166.

2 GENDER AND CULTURAL DIFFERENCES IN TOUCHING

A great deal of research has been directed at the question of who touches whom where. Most of it has attempted to address two basic questions: (1) Are there gender differences? Do men and women communicate through touch in the same way? Are men and women touched in the same way? (2) Are there cultural differences? Do people in widely different cultures communicate through touch in the same way?

GENDER DIFFERENCES

One of the most famous studies on gender differences was conducted by Sidney M. Jourard (1971), a summary of whose findings is presented in Figure 8.1. In the first figure, labeled "Body for Mother," we have the

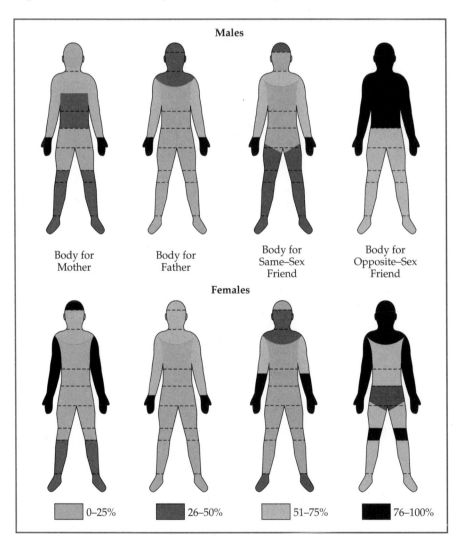

Males

Body for Mother   Body for Father   Body for Same–Sex Friend   Body for Opposite–Sex Friend

Females

0–25%   26–50%   51–75%   76–100%

Figure 8.1 The amount of touching of the various parts of the body as reported by male and female college students (adapted from S. M. Jourard, "An Exploratory Study of Body Accessibility," *British Journal of Social and Clinical Psychology 5*, 1966:221–231)

areas and frequency with which areas of a male college student's body were touched by his mother. The second figure records the areas and frequency with which these areas were touched by the student's father, and so on. The key within the figure indicates the percentage of students who reported being touched in these areas.

Jourard reports that touching and being touched differ little between men and women. Men touch and are touched as often and in the same places as women. The major exception to this is the touching behavior of mothers and fathers. Mothers touch children of both sexes and of all ages a great deal more than do fathers, who in many instances go no further than touching the hands of their children.

Other studies that have found differences between touching behavior in men and women seem to indicate that women touch more than men do. For example, women touch their fathers more than men do. Also, female babies are touched more than male babies. In an investigation of the wish to be held versus the wish to hold, women reported a greater

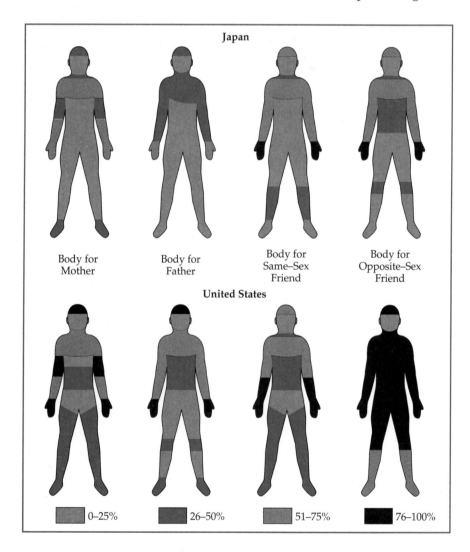

Figure 8.2 Areas and frequency of touching as reported by Japanese and United States college students (adapted from Dean C. Barnlund, "Communicative Styles in Two Cultures: Japan and the United States," in A. Kendon, R. M. Harris, and M. R. Key, eds., *Organization Behavior in Face-to-Face Interaction,* The Hague: Mouton, 1975)

desire to be held than to hold; and although men also report a desire to be held, it is not as intense as that of women. This, of course, fits in quite neatly with our cultural stereotypes of men being protectors (and therefore indicating a preference for holding) and women being protected (and therefore indicating a preference for being held).

A great deal more touching is reported among opposite-sex friends than among same-sex friends. Both male and female college students report that they touch and are touched more by their opposite-sex friends than by their same-sex friends. No doubt the strong societal bias against same-sex touching accounts, at least in part, for the greater prevalence of opposite-sex touching that most studies report. I suspect, however, that a great deal of touching goes on among same-sex friends, but goes unreported because many people are unaware of touching same-sex partners.

The Jourard study, replicated ten years later, found support for all Jourard's earlier findings, except that in the latter study both males and females were touched more by opposite-sex friends than in the earlier study.

CULTURAL DIFFERENCES

In a similar study, college students in Japan and in the United States were surveyed. The results, presented in Figure 8.2, make a particularly dramatic case for cross-cultural differences; students from the United States reported being touched twice as much as did students from Japan. In Japan, there is a strong taboo against strangers touching, and the Japanese are therefore especially careful to maintain sufficient distance.

Another obvious cross-cultural difference is in the Middle East, where same-sex touching in public is extremely common. Men will, for example, walk with their arms on each other's shoulders – a practice that would cause many raised eyebrows in the United States. Middle Easterners, Latin Americans, and southern Europeans touch each other while talking a great deal more often than do people from "noncontact" cultures – Asia and northern Europe, for example.

Even such seemingly minor nonverbal differences as these can create difficulties when members of different cultures interact. Northern Europeans or Japanese may be perceived as cold, distant, and uninvolved by southern Europeans, who in turn may be perceived as pushy, aggressive, and inappropriately intimate.

AFTER YOU READ

Task 1 Language focus: The passive

> **P**assive sentences are found frequently in academic discourse, so it is important to be able to recognize the passive and use it correctly.

There is, of course, a big difference in meaning between an active and a passive sentence. Compare for example:

X touches Y.   X is touched by Y.

In the first sentence, the verb is active. X, the subject, is the one who touches Y, and Y receives X's touch. In the second sentence, X is still the grammatical subject, but the verb is passive. It is Y who touches X and X who receives Y's touch.

According to the information in the text, decide if the active form of the verb or the passive form of the verb correctly completes the following sentences.

1 According to Jourard, mothers _____ their children more than fathers.
   a touch
   b are touched by

2 Fathers _____ their children as much as mothers.
   a do not touch
   b are not touched by

3 Women _____ their fathers more than men.
   a touch
   b are touched by

4 Female babies _____ more than male babies.
   a touch
   b are touched

5 Women prefer to _____.
   a hold
   b be held

6 According to the stereotype of women, they like to _____.
   a protect
   b be protected

7 Researchers _____ male and female touching behavior in the United States and Japan.
   a studied
   b were studied by

8 Middle Easterners may _____ people from "noncontact" cultures as being too intimate.
   a perceive
   b be perceived by

Task 2 Examining graphic material

> **R**emember that any graphic material (figures, diagrams, charts, and so on) carries important information and must be studied carefully, just like the text itself.

Look at Figure 8.1 in the text and answer questions 1a–e. Then look at Figure 8.2 in the text and answer questions 2a–e.

1 On which part(s) of the body:
   a is it most acceptable for people to touch each other?
   b do mothers touch their sons the same amount as they touch their daughters?
   c do fathers touch their daughters more than their sons?
   d do females touch each other most frequently?
   e do opposite-sex friends touch each other with about the same degree of frequency?

2 On which part(s) of the body:
   a do Japanese and American parents touch their children with about the same degree of frequency?
   b do Japanese parents touch their children more than American parents?
   c is it least acceptable for an American mother to touch her children?
   d is it most acceptable for a Japanese father to touch his children?
   e do same-sex friends in Japan and the United States touch each other with about the same degree of frequency?

Task 3 Writing: Using transitional expressions

Write sentences contrasting male and female, and Japanese and American touching behavior. Base your sentences on the information in Figures 8.1 and 8.2, and use these sentence structures to frame your answers. Note that Xs and Ys stand for groups of people being contrasted.

1 Whereas Xs _____, Ys _____.

> *Whereas Japanese mothers touch their children infrequently on the upper arm, American women tend to touch their children frequently on this part.*

2 Xs _____. However, Ys _____.
3 Xs _____. On the other hand, Ys _____.
4 Xs _____. By contrast, Ys _____.
5 One major difference between Xs and Ys is that Xs _____, whereas Ys _____.
6 When we compare Xs and Ys, we see that, whereas Xs _____, Ys _____.
7 Unlike Xs, we see that Ys _____.

PREPARING TO READ

Gathering data

> **D**oing some small-scale research and gathering data relating to the topic that you are going to read about helps provide a context for your reading.

1► Before reading this text, spend five minutes outside the classroom with a partner and secretly observe two people talking. Notice the following details:

Space: How far apart are the two people from each other?

Touch: Do they ever touch? Where? For how long?

Gestures: How do they use their hands and head?
                                How do they position their bodies?

Eye contact: How much do they look at each other? Is one person
                                making more eye contact than the other?

Facial expressions: What facial expressions do you observe?

2► Report back to the class on what you observed and what relationship you think the two people had. Explain your reasoning. Also, if possible, describe what you think they may have been talking about.

Predicting the content

According to this text, people create different amounts of distance between them depending on their relationships. The four different distances named in the text are:

  a intimate distance   *c* social distance
  b personal distance   *d* public distance

Which picture do you think represents people at each of these different distances?

NOW READ

Now read the text "Space Communication." When you finish, check to see if your predictions were correct and then turn to the tasks that begin on page 172.

3   SPACE COMMUNICATION

Edward T. Hall, in "A System for the Notation of Proxemic Behavior" (1963), defines **proxemics** as "the study of how man unconsciously structures microspace – the distance between men in the conduct of their daily transactions, the organization of space in his houses and buildings, and ultimately the layout of his town." In his analysis of the physical space between people in their interpersonal relationships, Hall (1966) distinguishes four distances that he feels define the type of relationship permitted. Each of these four distances has a close phase and a far phase, giving us a total of eight clearly identifiable distances. These four distances, according to Hall, correspond to the four major types of relationships: intimate, personal, social, and public.

proxemics
the study of how people manage space, particularly the distances between themselves and others in interpersonal relationships

INTIMATE DISTANCE

In intimate distance, ranging from the close phase of actual touching to the far phase of 6 to 18 inches, the presence of the other individual is unmistakable. Each individual experiences the sound, smell, and feel of the other's breath. The close phase is used for lovemaking and wrestling, for comforting and protecting. In the close phase, the muscles and the skin communicate, while actual verbalizations play a minor role. In this close phase, whispering, says Hall, has the effect of increasing the psychological distance between the two individuals. The far phase allows us to touch each other by extending our hands. The distance is so close that it is not considered proper for strangers in public, and because of the feeling of inappropriateness and discomfort (at least for some Americans), the eyes seldom meet but remain fixed on some remote object.

PERSONAL DISTANCE

Each of us, says Hall, carries a protective bubble defining our personal distance, which allows us to stay protected and untouched by others. In

Crowded subways force us to stand at a personal and even intimate distance from total strangers. What can you do to increase the psychological distance between you and other people in these situations?

the close phase of personal distance (1 to 2 feet) we can still hold or grasp each other, but only by extending our arms. We can then take into our protective bubble certain individuals – for example, loved ones. In the far phase (2 to 4 feet) two people can touch each other only if they both extend their arms. This far phase is the extent to which we can physically get our hands on things, hence it defines in one sense the limits of our physical control over others. Even at this distance we can see many of the fine details of an individual – the gray hairs, tooth stains, clothing lint, and so on. However, we can no longer detect body heat. At times we may detect breath odor, but generally at this distance etiquette demands that we direct our breath to some neutral corner so as not to offend.

At this distance we cannot perceive normal cologne or perfume. Thus it has been proposed that cologne has two functions. First, it serves to disguise the body odor or hide it; and second it serves to make clear the limit of the protective bubble around the individual. The bubble, defined by the perfume, signals that you may not enter beyond the point at which you can smell me.

SOCIAL DISTANCE

At the social distance, we lose the visual detail we had in the personal distance. The close phase (4 to 7 feet) is the distance at which we conduct impersonal business, the distance at which we interact at a social gathering. The far phase (7 to 12 feet) is the distance we stand when someone says, "Stand away so I can look at you." At this distance, business transactions have a more formal tone than when conducted in the close phase.

People sharing an office will arrange the space so that even though they are physically close, they feel psychologically distant.

In offices of high officials, the desks are positioned so that the individual is assured of at least this distance when dealing with clients. Unlike the intimate distance, where eye contact is awkward, the far phase of the social distance makes eye contact essential – otherwise communication is lost. The voice is generally louder than normal at this level, but shouting or raising the voice has the effect of reducing the social distance to a personal distance. It is at this distance we can work with people and yet not constantly interact with them. The social distance requires that a certain amount of space be available. In many instances, however, such distances are not available; yet it is necessary to keep social distance, psychologically if not physically. In order to achieve this, we attempt different arrangements with the furniture. In a small office, for example, people sharing an office might have their desks face in different directions so that each worker may stay separated from the other. Or they may position their desks against opposite walls so that each will feel psychologically alone in the office, and thus be able to maintain a social rather than a personal distance.

PUBLIC DISTANCE

In the close phase of public distance (12 to 15 feet), an individual seems protected by space. At this distance, one is able to take a defensive action should one be threatened. On a public bus or train, for example, we might keep at least this distance from a drunkard so that should anything happen, we could get away in time. Although at this distance we lose the fine details of the face and eyes, we are still close enough to see what is happening in case we need to take defensive action.

At the far phase (more than 25 feet) we see individuals not as separate individuals but as part of the whole setting. We automatically set approximately 30 feet around public figures who are of considerable importance and we seem to do this whether or not there are guards preventing us from entering this distance. This far phase is, of course, the distance from which actors perform on stage; consequently, their actions and voices have to be somewhat exaggerated.

AFTER YOU READ

Task 1 Note-taking: Creating grids

> **W**hen information in a text contains categories with contrasting characteristics, it is often possible to create a grid to display that information. If you can find a way to do this in your note-taking, it is always a good idea, because information displayed in this way is easy to review later for a test.

Look at the grid one student has created from the information in this text. Some of the details have been entered into the grid. Review the text and complete the grid with the missing details.

	distance in close phase	distance in far phase	typical relationship between people (in far phase)	example of what one can see or smell	voice level used
intimate distance			lovers		
personal distance		2–4 feet			■
social distance	4–7 feet			■	louder than normal
public distance				no fine details	

Task 2 Conducting an experiment

1▶ In this text, you have read about the distances people normally keep between each other in different situations. What happens when you do not follow these norms? Try this experiment to find out.

1 Stand next to another student in the class. Talk to each other about any topic. (Choose something neutral such as what you did or are planning to do over the weekend.) After a couple of minutes, stop. Do not move at all. Notice how close to each other you are standing. This distance should feel comfortable to both of you. Does it?

2 Take one half-step toward the other person and continue talking for another few minutes. Stop and discuss with your partner how you felt each talking at this distance.

3 Both of you take one full step back. Continue talking for another few minutes. Stop and discuss how the extra distance affected your feelings and the way in which you used your voice and eyes.

2▶ The amount of comfort you felt at different distances may have depended in part on whom you were talking to. Try the same experiment again, but this time choose someone of a different culture, sex, or level of friendship.

Follow-up: Writing about your experiment

Write about the experiment you performed in Task 2. Describe how you felt at each of the different distances and discuss any other changes you noticed in your nonverbal behavior.

PREPARING TO READ

Thinking about the topic

The main idea of this text is that you can make judgments about people according to the things that they own and the clothes that they wear. What can you tell about these three people from their appearance and possessions? What influenced your judgments?

Scanning

> **R**emember, when you scan a text, you do not read every word. Your eyes pass over the text, stopping only when you find the word or information you are looking for.

1➤ Scan the first part of this text and find the company brand names that are mentioned.

Brand name

_____	an American department store
_____	a German car company
_____	a famous American jeans company
_____	a very expensive brand of watch
_____	an Italian car company
_____	an Italian company famous for its shoes, handbags, and luggage

2➤ Scan the second part of this text and find the specific examples mentioned that may be given as gifts.

Gift

_____	something for a woman to wear
_____	something for someone to build body strength
_____	a piece of scientific equipment

NOW READ

Now read the text "Artifactual Communication." When you finish, turn to the tasks on page 176.

4   ARTIFACTUAL COMMUNICATION

Although we have concentrated on behaviors in this chapter, it would be a mistake to assume that all nonverbal communication takes place behaviorally. Numerous nonverbal messages are communicated by clothing and other artifacts, such as jewelry, makeup, buttons, the car you drive, the home you live in, the furniture you have and its arrangement, and in fact, just about every object with which you associate yourself. Your associations with an Alfa Romeo, Gucci leather, and cashmere sweaters say something very different from what your associations with a Volkswagen, vinyl, and polyester would say. A Rolex and a Timex may both give you the correct time, but each communicates differently about you. Whatever you wear (or do not wear) and what you are associated with (or are not associated with) will communicate something about you.

Often the gifts we give may carry an unconscious message.

We learn early to form impressions of people on the basis of their clothing. In a study by Michael Solomon (1986), children from the fourth and sixth grades rated wearers of a variety of types of jeans and shoes, in such dimensions as popularity, attractiveness, and friendliness. For example, when the children were shown wearers of three brands of jeans – Calvin Klein (designer type, high-priced), Levi Strauss (medium-priced), and Sears Toughskins (inexpensive), the children perceived the Levi Strauss wearers most favorably and the Sears wearers most negatively.

GIFTS AS NONVERBAL MESSAGES

A number of theorists have recently pointed out how we communicate even in our gift-giving. One type of gift has been referred to as the **Pygmalion gift**, that is, the gift that seems to be designed to change the person into what the donor wants the person to become. The husband who buys his wife sexy lingerie may be asking his wife to be sexy; the wife who buys her husband a weight-lifting machine may well be asking the same thing. The parent who repeatedly gives a child books or scientific equipment, such as a microscope, may be asking the child to be a scholar. The problem with some of these gifts is that the underlying motives – the underlying displeasures – may never be talked about and hence never resolved.

Pygmalion gift
a gift that communicates the gift-giver's desire for the person to change his or her personality or life-style

This is not to say that all gifts are motivated by negative aspects of our personalities, only to suggest that even in gift-giving there are messages communicated that are often overlooked and that often function below the level of conscious awareness. Such messages, however, may have considerable impact on the recipient, the donor, and the relationship itself (Dullea, 1981).

AFTER YOU READ

Task 1 Inferencing

> **W**riters often make you do some work in your reading. Not every-
> thing is directly stated or specific. Sometimes you may have to do
> your own inferencing or reasoning to make the author's ideas clear.

Discuss the answers to the questions below.

1 The author does not state this directly, but what is the difference between the
   items in column A and the items in column B?

A	*B*
an Alfa Romeo car	a Volkswagen car
cashmere	polyester
a Rolex watch	a Timex watch

2 Why did the children select the Levi Strauss wearers as being the most popular
   and attractive, and the Sears jeans wearers as the least attractive? The author does
   not explain this. Can you?

3 The author says that giving a "Pygmalion gift," such as sexy lingerie, weight-lifting
   equipment, or books suggests possible "underlying displeasures." What do you
   think is meant by this?

4 The author suggests that gifts are unconscious messages that may have considerable impact on the recipient (who receives the gift), the donor (who gives the gift),
   and their relationship. What sort of impact might the author have in mind?

Task 2 Personal writing

Without worrying about grammar or spelling, do some personal writing on the topic of
gifts. Use the following questions as a guide: Do you like to give and receive gifts? What
sorts of gifts do you like to give? What sorts of gifts do you like/not like to receive? Have
you ever received or given a "Pygmalion gift"? What was it?

CHAPTER 8 Writing assignment

Choose one of the following topics as your chapter writing assignment.

1 Explain how differences in the degree of intimacy between two people might affect
   the physical distance they keep between them and when and where they might
   touch each other.

2 Discuss how our possessions tell a lot about who we are and what our values are.

3 Evaluate how you might use the information in this chapter in your daily life.

UNIT 5

Interpersonal Relationships

In this unit we study two important kinds of relationships that we develop during our lives. In Chapter 9, we read about friendship, specifically about how and why people establish friendships and what they do to develop and maintain those friendships. In Chapter 10, we read about love. We examine the question of why we become attracted to some people, but not to others, and we learn that there are many different types of love and ways of loving.

PREVIEWING THE UNIT

Before you read a unit (or chapter) of a textbook, it is a good idea to preview the contents page and think about the topics that will be covered.

Read the contents page for Unit 5 and answer the following questions with a partner.

Chapter 9: Friendship

1➤ How should you behave the first time you meet someone whom you would like to get to know better? What should you talk about? The first two sections of Chapter 9 focus on these questions.

Imagine you are meeting someone for the first time. Decide which of the following topics would be good to talk about (check *Yes*), and which would not (check *No*). When you finish, decide which topic would be the best choice, and which the worst. Give reasons.

		Yes	*No*
1	Some neutral topic, like the weather or the traffic	❏	❏
2	Some controversial topic, like politics or religion	❏	❏
3	A personal problem that you have	❏	❏
4	A personal problem that the other person has	❏	❏
5	Something the other person is wearing or carrying	❏	❏
6	Something that you are wearing or carrying	❏	❏

2➤ In the final two sections of this chapter, you will read about friendship. Think of as many different ways as you can to finish this sentence:

"I most need a friend when . . ."

Chapter 10: Love

1➤ In the first two sections of Chapter 10, you will read about why we become attracted to certain people, but not to others. Here are two proverbs from the reading in Section 2, "Complementarity." Discuss which one you think is more often true and why.

Birds of a feather flock together. (In other words, we are usually more attracted to people who are similar to ourselves.)

Opposites attract. (In other words, we are usually more attracted to people who are different from ourselves.)

2➤ The last two sections of this chapter deal with different types of love. How would you define the difference between "love" and "friendship"?

UNIT CONTENTS

PREPARING TO READ

Thinking about the topic

This text describes the steps involved in beginning a conversation with someone that you might like to get to know. Discuss the following questions with a partner.

1 What are some positive and negative aspects of starting a conversation with a stranger in the following places?

a library	a party
a disco	a bar
a museum or art gallery	a train station
a classroom	a bus stop

2 An "opening line" is the first thing you say when you approach a stranger and try to start a conversation. What would be a good opening line in each of the places mentioned above?

3 Would you feel uncomfortable initiating a conversation with a stranger? Why? Would you feel uncomfortable having a stranger initiate a conversation with you? Why? If the answer to these questions is "It depends," explain what it depends on.

Highlighting

> **H**ighlighting key terms that appear in bold print or italics and then finding the accompanying definitions of those terms is a good pre-reading strategy. It gives you a good idea of what is going to be important in a text before you do a close reading.

1► Scan the text for the following words and phrases and highlight them.

- qualifiers
- an integrating topic
- free information
- a come-on self

2► Now find the definitions of these terms and highlight them, using a different-colored marker.

3► Compare what you highlighted with another student in the class.

NOW READ

Now read the text "Initiating Relationships." When you finish, turn to the tasks on page 183.

CHAPTER 9

Friendship

1 INITIATING RELATIONSHIPS

Perhaps the most difficult and yet the most important aspect of relationship development is the process of initiating relationships – meeting the person and presenting yourself. Murray Davis, in "Intimate Relations" (1973), notes that the first encounter consists of six steps, similar to those represented in Figure 9.1, "The process of asking for a date."

EXAMINE THE QUALIFIERS

The first step is to examine the *qualifiers*, those qualities that make the individual you wish to encounter an appropriate choice. Some qualifiers are manifest or open to easy inspection, such as beauty, style of clothes, jewelry, and the like. Other qualifiers are latent or hidden from easy inspection, such as personality, health, wealth, talent, intelligence, and the like. Qualifiers tell us something about who the person is and help us to decide if we wish to pursue this initial encounter.

DETERMINE CLEARANCE

Try to determine if this person is available for an encounter. Is the person wearing a wedding ring? Does the person seem to be waiting for someone else?

OPEN THE ENCOUNTER

Open the encounter, both nonverbally and verbally. Davis suggests that we look for two things: (1) a topic that will interest the other person (and you) and that could be drawn out of the opener and (2) indications by the

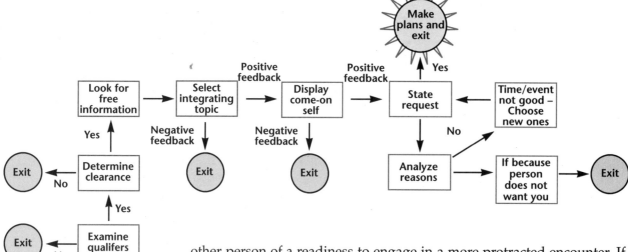

Figure 9.1 The process of asking for a date (adapted from DeVito, 1989)

other person of a readiness to engage in a more protracted encounter. If yes/no answers are given to your questions or if eye contact is not maintained, then you have some pretty good indication that this person is not open to an extended encounter with you at this time. If, on the other hand, the person responds at length or asks you questions in return, then you have some feedback that says "Continue!"

SELECT AN INTEGRATING TOPIC

An *integrating topic* is one that will interest the other person and you, and will serve to integrate or unite the two of you. Generally, such topics are found through an analysis of free information and questions and answers. Look, therefore, for *free information* – information about the person that you can see or that is dropped into the conversation. For example, a college ring or jacket, a beeper, or a uniform will tell you something about the person and will suggest a possible topic of conversation. Similarly, a casual remark may include the person's occupation or area of study or sports interests – all of which can be used as take-off points for further interaction. Look and listen, therefore, for the free information that will enable you to continue the interaction and that will suggest additional communication topics. Further, ask questions (none that are too prying, of course) to discover more about this person and to communicate your interest.

CREATE A FAVORABLE IMPRESSION

Display what is called a *come-on self*, a part of you that is inviting, engaging, and otherwise interesting to another person. Display a part of you that will make the other person want to continue the encounter.

ESTABLISH A SECOND MEETING

If you and your new partner seem to be getting along, then a second meeting should be established. This may vary from a very general type of meeting ("Do you always eat here on Fridays?") to a very specific type of meeting ("How about going to the beach next Saturday?").

AFTER YOU READ

Task 1 Reading for detail

Number the headings in this text, 1–6. Each heading describes one of the six steps that can occur in a first encounter. In which step might each of the following behaviors occur? Write the heading number in the blank.

_____ *a* You smile a lot and try to be charming.
_____ *b* You try to keep the conversation about the other person.
_____ *c* You look to see if the other person is waiting for someone else.
_____ *d* You take a close look at the other person's clothes and style.
_____ *e* You turn the conversation to talk about the future.
_____ *f* You listen to see if the other person answers you at length.

Task 2 Building vocabulary: Guessing meaning from context

Use the context to work out what the words in bold probably mean.

> Some qualifiers are **manifest** or open to easy inspection such as beauty, style of clothes, jewelry, **and the like**. Other qualifiers are **latent** or hidden from easy inspection such as personality, health, wealth, talent, intelligence, and the like.

manifest _____

and the like _____

latent _____

> If yes/no answers are given to your questions or if **eye contact is not maintained**, then you have some pretty good indication that this person is not open to an **extended** encounter with you at this time. If, on the other hand, the person **responds at length** or asks you questions in return, then you have some feedback that says "Continue!"

to maintain eye contact _____

extended _____

to respond at length _____

> Further, ask questions (none that are too **prying**, of course) to discover more about this person and to communicate your interest. . . . If you and your new partner seem **to be getting along**, then a second **meeting should be established**. This may vary from a very general type of meeting ("Do you always eat here on Fridays?") to a very specific type of meeting ("How about going to the beach next Saturday?").

prying _____

to get along _____

to establish a meeting _____

PREPARING TO READ

Examining graphic material

> Before reading a text, it is a good idea to examine any graphic material. Simply looking at the photographs and illustrations in a text can be helpful.

Look at the picture in the text and discuss the following questions with a partner.

1 Where are these two people?

2 How well do you think they know each other?

3 How interested is the man in talking to the woman? How can you tell from his body language?

4 How interested is the woman in the man? How can you tell from her body language?

Predicting the content

1➤ This text offers suggestions for how to act during a first encounter with a stranger. Predict whether the author will recommend (write *R*) or not recommend (write *NR*) the following behaviors.

_____ *1* Keep your arms crossed over your chest.
_____ *2* Get as close to the other person as possible.
_____ *3* Give all your attention to the other person.
_____ *4* Try not to look into the other person's eyes.
_____ *5* When the other person gives you a positive sign, you should also give a positive sign back, like a smile.
_____ *6* After you have made contact nonverbally, it is best not to wait too long before you start talking.
_____ *7* Introduce yourself simply by saying, "Hi, my name is . . ."
_____ *8* Try to keep the conversation mostly about you, so the other person can learn as much about you as possible.
_____ *9* If you see something you like in the other person, give a compliment, for example, say, "I really like your shoes."
_____ *10* Quickly start talking about your very deepest feelings.
_____ *11* Talk about people, places, leisure activities that you both know about.
_____ *12* Ask many questions that begin, "Are you?", "Do you?", "Have you?", and so on.

2➤ Compare answers with a partner.

NOW READ

Now read the text "The Nonverbal and Verbal First Encounter." When you finish, check to see if your predictions were correct. Then turn to the tasks on page 187.

2 THE NONVERBAL AND VERBAL FIRST ENCOUNTER

Here are a few suggestions for how to act during the first encounter. Although they are divided into the "nonverbal encounter" and the "verbal encounter," recognize that these must be integrated for any effective encounter to occur.

THE NONVERBAL ENCOUNTER

Nonverbal communication concerns every aspect of yourself that sends messages to another person. On the basis of these messages, the other person forms an impression of you – an impression that will be quickly and firmly established.

1 Establish eye contact. Eye contact is the first nonverbal signal to send. The eyes communicate an awareness of and interest in the other person.
2 While maintaining eye contact, smile and further signal your interest in and your positive response to this other person.
3 Concentrate your focus. The rest of the room should be nonverbally shut off from awareness. Be careful, however, that you do not focus so directly as to make the person uncomfortable.
4 Establish physical closeness, or at least lessen the physical distance between the two of you. Approach, but not to the point of discomfort, so that your interest in making contact is obvious.
5 Throughout this nonverbal encounter, maintain a posture that communicates an openness, a willingness to enter into interaction with the other person. Hands crossed over the chest or clutched around your stomach are exactly the kind of postures that you want to avoid. These are often interpreted to signal an unwillingness to let others enter your space.
6 Respond visibly. Assuming that your nonverbal communication is returned, respond to it visibly with a smile, a head nod, a wink.
7 Reinforce positive behaviors. Reinforce those behaviors of the other person that signal interest and a reciprocal willingness to make contact. Reinforce these by responding positively to them; again, nod or smile or somehow indicate your favorable reaction.
8 Avoid overexposure. Nonverbal communication works to make contact or to signal interest, but it can cause problems if it is excessive or if it is not followed by more direct communication. Consequently, if you intend to make verbal contact, do so after a relatively short time or wait until another time.

THE VERBAL ENCOUNTER

1 Introduce yourself. Try to avoid trite and clichéd opening lines. Do not become identified with, "Haven't I seen you here before?"

nonverbal communication
messages communicated by your eyes, face, and body, also by your clothes and other possessions you display

The body language of these two people suggests that a successful first encounter is in progress.

Actually, these openers are legitimate and would be more than appropriate if others understood that opening lines are merely ways of saying "Hello." But many do not; many think that these lines are a measure of your intelligence and wit. Given that sorry state of affairs, it is probably best to simply say, "Hi, my name is Pat."

2 Focus the conversation on the other person. Get the other person involved in talking about himself or herself: No one enjoys talking about anything more. Also, it will provide you with an opportunity to learn something about the person you want to get to know.

3 Compliment the other person; be sincere but complimentary and positive. If you cannot find anything to compliment the person about, then it is probably wise to reassess your interest in this person and perhaps move on.

4 Be energetic. No one likes a lethargic, slow-moving, nondynamic partner. Demonstrate your high energy level by responding facially with appropriate effect, smiling, talking in a varied manner, being flexible with your body posture and gestures, asking questions as appropriate, and otherwise demonstrating that you are really here.

5 Stress the positives. In the discussion of interpersonal effectiveness, it was noted that positiveness was one of the major qualities of effectiveness. It also contributes to a positive first impression simply because we like and are attracted to a positive more than a negative person.

6 Avoid negative and too intimate self-disclosures. Enter a relationship gradually and gracefully. Disclosures should come gradually and along with reciprocal disclosures. Anything too intimate or too negative early in the relationship will create a negative image. If you cannot resist self-disclosing, then try to stick to the positives and to those matters that would not be considered overly intimate.

7 Establish commonalities. Seek to discover in your interaction those things you have in common with the other person – attitudes, interests, personal qualities, third parties, places, and so on.

8 Avoid yes/no questions, yes/no answers, and rapid-fire questions. Ask questions that are open-ended, questions that the receiver may answer at some length. Similarly, respond with answers more complete than simply yes or no. Be careful, too, that your questions do not appear to be an interrogation.

AFTER YOU READ

Task 1 Dramatizing the text

> **A**n effective way to determine whether you have fully understood new information is to apply that information in role play.

1▶ Work in groups of three. One student will be an observer. The other two students will act out the following situation:

Two students are seated next to each other, waiting for their professor to come into class. They do not know each other. One of the students wants to get to know the other student and initiates a conversation.

2▶ After the conversation, the observer will report on how well the initiator used nonverbal and verbal strategies in engaging the other student in a first encounter conversation.

Task 2 Writing a paragraph

> **O**rganizing new information into a paragraph that includes a few key examples is an excellent way to deepen your understanding of new subject matter.

1▶ Using information from the text, write a paragraph on one of the following topics.

1 Nonverbal behaviors you should avoid when you first meet someone whom you would like to get to know

2 Nonverbal behaviors you should use when you first meet someone whom you would like to get to know

3 Verbal behaviors you should avoid when you first meet someone whom you would like to get to know

4 Verbal behaviors you should use when you first meet someone whom you would like to get to know

2▶ Read over what you have written and ask yourself these questions: Is it clear? Are there transitional expressions to guide the reader through the text? Is it well organized? Is there a topic sentence and a concluding sentence? Are there enough examples to support the topic sentence? Is the use of language correct? (Check spelling, grammar, and vocabulary use.)

3▶ Now rewrite your paragraph and improve it in any way possible.

PREPARING TO READ

Thinking about the topic

Discuss the following questions with a partner.

1 How would you define "a friend"?

2 Make a list of the different activities that you have done with friends in the past week. Then compare your answer with the list in Figure A on page 195 in Section 4, which shows the ten most frequently mentioned activities that people say they share with their friends.

3 How many close friends do you have? Do you have a close friend of the opposite sex?

Predicting the content

In this text, five values, or rewards, of friendship are described. The box on the right contains glosses that will help you understand the names for these five values.

a a utility value
b an affirmation value
c an ego-support value
d a stimulation value
e a security value

> utility: usefulness
> affirmation: statement of truth
> ego: sense of one's importance
> stimulation: the source of new and interesting ideas
> security: a sense of being safe

1➤ The following examples are given in the text to illustrate the five different friendship values. Before reading the text, try to match each example to one of the values of friendship. Write the letter in the blank.

_____ *1* A friend enables us to come into contact with issues and concepts with which we were not previously familiar – modern art, foreign cultures, new foods. . . .

_____ *2* A friend may, for example, help us to recognize our leadership abilities, our athletic prowess, or our sense of humor.

_____ *3* A friend does nothing to hurt the other person or to emphasize or call attention to the other person's inadequacies or weaknesses.

_____ *4* We may, for example, become friends with someone who is particularly bright because such a person might assist us in getting better grades, in solving our personal problems, or in getting a better job.

_____ *5* Friends enable us more easily to view ourselves as worthy and competent individuals.

2➤ Compare answers with a partner.

NOW READ

Now read the text "Friendship Functions." When you finish, check to see if you matched the examples and friendship values correctly. Then turn to the tasks on page 191.

3 FRIENDSHIP FUNCTIONS

NEED SATISFACTION

Friendships develop and are maintained to satisfy our needs. Selecting friends on the basis of need satisfaction is similar to choosing a marriage partner, an employee, or any person who may be in a position to satisfy our needs. Thus, for example, if we have the need to be the center of attention or to be popular, we choose friends who fulfill these needs – that is, people who allow us, and even encourage us, to be the center of attention or who tell us, verbally and nonverbally, that we are popular. As we grow older or develop in different ways, our needs change, and in many instances old friends are dropped from our close circle to be replaced by new friends who better serve our new needs.

friendship
an interpersonal relationship between two persons that is mutually productive and characterized by mutual positive regard

FIVE FRIENDSHIP VALUES

Interpersonal researcher Paul H. Wright (1978, 1984) has identified more specifically the needs that we seek to have satisfied through friendships. We establish and maintain friendships, Wright observes, because they provide us with certain "direct rewards."

1 *Friends have a utility value.* A friend may have special talents, skills, or resources that may prove useful to us in achieving our specific goals and needs. We may, for example, become friends with someone who is particularly bright because such a person might assist us in getting better grades, in solving our personal problems, or in getting a better job.

2 *Friends have an affirmation value.* The behavior of a friend toward us acts as a mirror that serves to affirm our personal value and enables us to recognize our attributes. A friend may, for example, help us to recognize more clearly our leadership abilities, our athletic prowess, or our sense of humor.

3 *Friends have an ego-support value.* By behaving in a supportive, encouraging, and helpful manner, friends enable us more easily to view ourselves as worthy and competent individuals.

4 *Friends have a stimulation value.* A friend introduces us to new ideas and new ways of seeing the world and helps us to expand our world view. A friend enables us to come into contact with issues and concepts with which we were not previously familiar – modern art, foreign cultures, new foods, and hundreds of other new, different, and stimulating things.

5 *Friends have a security value.* A friend does nothing to hurt the other person or to emphasize or call attention to the other person's inadequacies or weaknesses. Because of this security value, friends can interact freely and openly without having to worry about betrayal or negative responses.

It is true that we need friends to help us when we are down, but we also need them to share our good news with us.

PLEASURE AND PAIN FUNCTIONS

The other function of friendship is to maximize pleasure and minimize pain. This is actually a special case of the need-satisfaction function.

If you were to ask people to complete the statement "I most need a friend when . . . ," they would probably answer in one of two ways. One would be to say, "I most need a friend when I'm down," "I most need a friend when I'm feeling sorry for myself," or "I most need a friend when I'm depressed." Such statements exemplify the function that a friendship can serve when it helps us to avoid or lessen pain. We want a friend to be around when we are feeling down so that he or she will make us feel a little better, lift our spirits, or in some way alleviate the pain we are feeling.

The other way to complete the statement would be to say, "I most need a friend when I'm happy," "when I want to share my good news," or "when I want someone to enjoy something with me." These statements typify the general function friendships serve to augment one's pleasure. A great part of the pleasure in winning a game, in receiving good news, and in experiencing good fortune is in telling someone else about it and in many cases sharing it with them.

AFTER YOU READ

Task 1 Building vocabulary: Synonyms

> **G**ood writers try to vary their use of language in a text. When they have to express the same idea more than once, they will often use synonyms to avoid repeating themselves. Being aware of this may help you, since ideas that are expressed in language that you do not understand in one place in the text might be found elsewhere in the text in words that you do understand.

1▸ Look in the text for the expressions in the left hand column. Use the headings from the text to help you find the part of the text where they appear. Then find another expression in the text with a similar meaning. Write the missing word in the blank in the right hand column.

Need Satisfaction	
1 to fulfill needs	to _____ our needs
2 to select friends	to _____ friends
Five Friendship Values	
3 to establish friendships	to ____ friends with people
4 to assist us in doing something	to_____ us to do something
Pleasure and Pain Functions	
5 to augment one's pleasure	to _____ pleasure
6 to alleviate the pain	to _____ pain
7 to be down	to be _____

2▸ Compare answers with a partner.

Task 2 Personal writing

> **W**riting frequently in a private journal helps students overcome their fears of writing in a second language. Writing in a private journal about how a topic affects you personally is also a great way to deepen your understanding of a text.

In this text, you read about different friendship values and the functions friendship can serve. Think about your own friends. To what extent do your personal experiences support the ideas expressed in this text? Choose one of the five friendship values and write about a personal example to illustrate that value.

PREPARING TO READ

Thinking about the topic

In the final sentence of this text, the author mentions intercultural friendships. Discuss the following questions about friendship with your classmates.

1 Why might it be difficult to make friends with someone from another culture?

2 Do you have any friends from other cultures? If yes, how did you meet them and get to know them?

3 What could you do to increase your chances of meeting and making friends with someone from a different culture?

Examining graphic material

> **S**kimming through any figures or tables in a text before reading it will **a**id the reading process. You will get an idea of what the text is about, which should help you read more accurately.

In Figure 9.2 the author has listed in general terms some rules that are important for maintaining a friendship. Work with a partner and think of a situation that illustrates how to follow each rule. Here is an example of what you might say to illustrate Rule 1, "Stand up for Friend in his or her absence":

> Okay, for Rule 1, let's say someone is criticizing your friend when he or she is not there, they are saying that your friend doesn't like to spend money. You should defend your friend by saying that he or she is often very generous, and by giving some examples.

NOW READ

Now read the text "Friendship Rules. " When you finish, turn to the tasks on page 195.

4   FRIENDSHIP RULES

Recently, interpersonal researchers have sought to conceptualize friendship as rule-governed behavior and have attempted to identify the rules that friends consider important in maintaining their relationships.

The most important friendship rules identified by interpersonal researchers Michael Argyle and Monika Henderson (1984) are presented in Figure 9.2. When these rules are followed, the friendship is strong and mutually satisfying. In examining these rules, try to identify additional rules that you consider important in your own friendships.

> 1 Stand up for Friend in his or her absence.
> 2 Share information and feelings about successes.
> 3 Demonstrate emotional support.
> 4 Trust each other; confide in each other.
> 5 Offer to help Friend in time of need.
> 6 Try to make Friend happy when you and Friend are together.

Figure 9.2 Six rules for maintaining a friendship (based on Michael Argyle and Monika Henderson, "The rules of friendship," *Journal of Social and Personal Relationships* 1, June 1984: 211–237)

Figure 9.3 presents the abuses that are most significant in breaking up a friendship, also identified by Argyle and Henderson. Note that some of the rules for maintaining a friendship directly correspond to the abuses that break up friendships. For example, it is important to "show emotional support" to maintain a friendship, but when emotional support is not shown, the friendship will prove less satisfying and may well break

> 1 Be intolerant of Friend's friends.
> 2 Criticize Friend in public.
> 3 Discuss confidences between yourself and Friend with others.
> 4 Don't display any positive regard for Friend.
> 5 Don't demonstrate any positive support for Friend.
> 6 Nag Friend.
> 7 Don't trust or confide in Friend.
> 8 Don't volunteer to help Friend in time of need.
> 9 Be jealous or critical of Friend's other relationships.

Figure 9.3 How to break up a friendship (based on Michael Argyle and Monika Henderson, "The rules of friendship," *Journal of Social and Personal Relationships* 1, June 1984: 211–237)

Making friends with someone from another culture is not always easy; the rules of friendship may be different from one culture to another.

up. The general assumption here is that friendships break down when a significant friendship rule is violated.

Discovering the rules of friendship will serve a number of useful functions. Ideally, it will enable us to identify successful versus destructive friendship behavior. Thus, we will be better able to teach the social skills involved in friendship development and maintenance. Furthermore, these rules will help us to pinpoint in relatively specific terms what went wrong when a friendship breaks up and enable us possibly to repair the relationship. Finally, since the rules of friendship vary somewhat from one culture to another, it is helpful to identify the rules that are unique for each culture so that **intercultural friendships** may be more effectively developed and maintained.

intercultural friendship
friendship between people from different cultural backgrounds or countries, where friendship rules may be different

AFTER YOU READ

Task 1 Writing about information in figures

1▸ In the text, Figures 9.2 and 9.3 are introduced in the following language:

The most important friendship rules . . . are presented in Figure 9.2.

Figure 9.3 presents the abuses that are most significant in breaking up a friendship.

Use the same sentence structures to introduce Figure A below.

2▸ To draw attention to details in a figure, you can use these constructions:

Note that . . .   It is interesting to note that . . .   It is worth noting that . . .

Use these constructions to draw attention to details that you find worth noting in Figure A and also Figures 9.2 and 9.3 in the text.

> 1 Had an intimate talk
> 2 Had a friend ask you to do something for him or her
> 3 Went to dinner in a restaurant
> 4 Asked your friend to do something for you
> 5 Had a meal together at home or at your friend's home
> 6 Went to a movie, play, or concert
> 7 Went drinking together
> 8 Went shopping
> 9 Participated in sports
> 10 Watched a sporting event

Figure A The ten most frequently identified activities shared with friends (based on Mary Brown Parlee and the editors of *Psychology Today*, "The friendship bond," *Psychology Today* 13, October 1979: 43–54, 113)

Task 2 Personal writing

Describe a friendship that is over. Which of the rules of friendship were broken? What did you or your friend do that caused the relationship to end?

CHAPTER 9 Writing assignment

Choose one of the following topics as your chapter writing assignment.

1 Analyze a friendship that you have. Write about how the two of you met, what functions your friendship serves, and what you do to maintain your friendship. Use the concepts presented in this chapter in your analysis.

2 Imagine that someone who has studied this chapter is going to live in your country. What would you advise them about how to meet people, make friends, and maintain a friendship, that might be different from the information in this chapter?

3 Discuss how the information in this chapter may influence the way you behave with your friends and how you act when you meet people.

PREPARING TO READ

Personalizing the topic

> **T**hinking about your personal connections to a topic before you read about it will help you absorb new information on that topic.

1➤ Ask and answer the following questions with a partner. Use the structures that follow each question to help you frame your answer.

1 Which people in public life, for example, movie stars, singers, athletes, and TV personalities, do you find attractive?

I find _____ very attractive.

2 What sort of men or women are you attracted to? Give as much detail as possible, for example, eye color, type of hair, height, nationality, intelligence, values, and so on.

I am (very) attracted to men/women who _____.

I find men/women who _____ (very) attractive.

3 What sort of men or women do you find unattractive? Give details as above.

I am not (at all) attracted to men who _____.

I don't find men/women who _____ (very) attractive.

2➤ According to this text, we are often attracted to "mirror images of ourselves." Consider your descriptions of people that you find attractive. Discuss with your partner to what extent these descriptions could also be descriptions of yourself.

NOW READ

Now read the text "Similarity." When you finish, turn to the tasks on page 199.

CHAPTER 10

Love

1 SIMILARITY

If people could construct their mates, the mates would look, act, and think very much like themselves. By being attracted to people like ourselves, we are in effect validating ourselves, saying to ourselves that we are worthy of being liked, that we are attractive. Although there are exceptions, we generally like people who are similar to ourselves in nationality, race, ability, physical characteristics, intelligence, attitudes, and so on. We are often attracted to mirror images of ourselves.

THE MATCHING HYPOTHESIS

If you were to ask a group of friends, "To whom are you attracted?" they would probably name very attractive people; in fact, they would probably name the most attractive people they know. But if we were to observe these friends, we would find that they go out with and establish relationships with people who are quite similar to themselves in terms of physical attractiveness. Useful in this connection is the **matching hypothesis**, which states that although we may be attracted to the most physically attractive people, we date and mate with people who are similar to ourselves in physical attractiveness. Intuitively, this too seems satisfying. In some cases, however, we notice discrepancies; we notice an old person dating an attractive younger partner or an unattractive person with a handsome partner. In these cases, we will probably find that the less attractive partner possesses some quality that compensates for

matching hypothesis
the belief that people form relationships with others who are as physically attractive as themselves

These two people seem to illustrate the matching hypothesis.

the lack of physical attractiveness. Prestige, money, intelligence, power, and various personality characteristics are obvious examples of qualities that may compensate for being less physically attractive.

ATTITUDE SIMILARITY

Similarity is especially important when it comes to attitudes. We are particularly attracted to people who have attitudes similar to our own, who like what we like, and who dislike what we dislike. The more significant the attitude, the more important the similarity. For example, it would not make much difference if the attitudes of two people toward food or furniture differed (though even these can at times be significant), but it would be of great significance if their attitudes toward children or religion or politics were very disparate. Marriages between people with great and salient dissimilarities are more likely to end in divorce than are marriages between people who are very much alike.

Generally, we maintain balance with ourselves by liking people who are similar to us and who like what we like. It is psychologically uncomfortable to like people who do not like what we like or to dislike people who like what we like. Our attraction for similarity enables us to achieve psychological balance or comfort. The person who likes what we like in effect tells us that we are right to like what we like. Even after an examination it is helpful to find people who wrote the same answers we did. Notice the next time you have an examination how you prefer the company of others who have given the same answers as you!

AFTER YOU READ

Task 1 Reading for main ideas

The sentences below come from the text. Which of these sentences:

   a gives the main idea for the whole text?
   b gives the main idea for the first part of the text?
   c gives the main idea for the second part of the text?

_____ *1* Our attraction for similarity enables us to achieve psychological balance and comfort.

_____ *2* Although we may be attracted to the most physically attractive people, we date and mate with people who are similar to ourselves in physical attractiveness.

_____ *3* Marriages between people with great and salient dissimilarities are more likely to end in divorce than are marriages between people who are very much alike.

_____ *4* We are particularly attracted to people who have attitudes similar to our own, who like what we like, and who dislike what we dislike.

_____ *5* Although there are exceptions, we generally like people who are similar to ourselves. . . .

Task 2 Writing a one-sentence summary

> Sometimes a short text can be summarized in one sentence. Writing a one-sentence summary is a useful exercise. It helps you focus on what is really important in a text and also forces you to be concise and precise in your writing.

Write a one-sentence summary of this text. Include the following three words:

- similar
- attracted
- attitude

Task 3 Personal writing

Describe the qualities of people to whom you are usually attracted. Consider physical characteristics, intelligence, abilities, attitudes, nationality, and values.

PREPARING TO READ

Personalizing the topic

Do you think of yourself as shy but wish you were self-confident? Do you envy people who can make other people laugh? Write down five personal qualities or characteristics that you do not possess, but wish you did. These could be physical characteristics, personality characteristics, intellectual or athletic abilities, and so on. Begin your sentences:

I wish I were . . .

I wish I could . . .

I wish I had . . .

NOW READ

Now read the text "Complementarity." When you finish, do the tasks below.

AFTER YOU READ

Task 1 Thinking critically about the text

1➤ According to Theodore Reik, whose work is cited in this text, those qualities that you wish you had are also the qualities of the people you fall in love with. Look back at the sentences you wrote in "Personalizing the Topic." Do they support Reik's theory? Using these sentences as evidence, discuss with a partner whether you think Reik's theory is valid.

2➤ According to the matching hypothesis, we are more likely to be attracted to people who are similar to us. The complementarity principle says that we are attracted to people who are different from us. Which theory does the author imply is better supported by the evidence? Underline those parts of the text that support your answer.

Task 2 Building vocabulary: Antonyms

If it is true that "opposites attract," whom would the following people be attracted to? The answers can all be found in the text.

1 A dominant person would be attracted to a(n) _____ person.

2 A shy person would be attracted to a(n) _____.

3 A submissive person would be attracted to a(n) _____ person.

4 A witty person would be attracted to a(n) _____ person.

5 A man would be attracted to a(n) _____.

2   COMPLEMENTARITY

Although many people would argue that "Birds of a feather flock together," others would argue that "Opposites attract." This latter concept is the principle of **complementarity**. Take, for example, the individual who is extremely dogmatic. Would this person be attracted to people who are high in dogmatism or to those who are low in dogmatism? The similarity principle predicts that this person will be attracted to those who are like him or her (that is, high in dogmatism), while the complementarity principle predicts that this person will be attracted to those who are unlike him or her (that is, low in dogmatism).

It has been found that people are attracted to others who are dissimilar only in certain situations. For example, the submissive student may get along especially well with an aggressive teacher but may not get along with an aggressive spouse. The dominant wife may get along with a submissive husband but may not relate well to submissive colleagues. Theodore Reik, in *A Psychologist Looks at Love*, argues that we fall in love with people who possess characteristics that we do not possess and that we actually envy. The introvert, for example, if displeased with being shy, might be attracted to an extrovert.

There seems to be intuitive support for both complementarity and similarity, and certainly neither can be ruled out in terms of exerting significant influence on interpersonal attraction. The experimental evidence, however, favors similarity. Glenn Wilson and David Nias, in *The Mystery of Love* (1976), review evidence demonstrating that similarity in attitudes, physical attractiveness, self-esteem, race, religion, age, and social class increase attraction and therefore support the similarity theory.

Complementarity finds less support. The most obvious instance of complementarity is found in the fact that most persons are heterosexual and are attracted to persons of the opposite sex. One of the most interesting supports for complementarity appears in the finding that when one person in a relationship is "witty," the other person is "placid." It seems so much easier being witty with a placid listener than with a competing wit – something we have probably all observed in our own interpersonal relationships.

complementarity principle
the concept that people are attracted to those who are different from themselves

While research seems to favor the matching hypothesis, there are plenty of partners who are physically very different from each other.

PREPARING TO READ

Building vocabulary: Learning word clusters

> **R**emember that the more words you already know relating to a topic, the easier it is to read about that topic.

Read the following words or phrases taken from the text. They all cluster around or relate in some way to the topic of love. Then read the sentences that follow. For each sentence, find three words or phrases that may complete the sentence. Write the corresponding letters in the blanks.

a mate
b intensity
c excitement
d obsession
e break up
f erotic
g passion
h agree upon a long-term commitment

i jealousy
j lover
k possessiveness
l establish a relationship
m hedonistic
n partner
o sensual

1 In a relationship there are two people – you and your _____ _____ _____.

2 A strong negative emotion that may be felt by one person in the relationship is _____ _____ _____.

3 A(n) _____ _____ _____ experience is one involving strong physical or sexual feelings.

4 After knowing each other for a certain amount of time, two people may _____ _____ _____.

5 _____ _____ _____ may be described as a strong positive emotion felt in a relationship.

NOW READ

Now read the text "Types of Love." When you finish, turn to the tasks that begin on page 206.

3 TYPES OF LOVE

LUDUS: ENTERTAINMENT AND EXCITEMENT

Ludus love is experienced as a game. The *ludic lover* sees love as fun, a game to be played. The better he or she can play the game, the more the love is enjoyed. To the ludic lover, love is not to be taken too seriously; emotions are to be held in check lest they get out of hand and make trouble; passions never rise to the point at which they get out of control. Ludic love is a self-controlled love – a love that the lover carefully manages and controls rather than allowing it to control him or her.

Ludic lovers change partners frequently. Perhaps because love is a game, sexual fidelity is not something that is of major importance in a ludic love relationship. The ludic lover expects his or her partner to have had (and probably to have in the future) other partners and does not get upset if this happens occasionally during their relationship.

The ludic lover retains a partner only so long as the partner is interesting and amusing. When the partner is no longer interesting enough, it is time to change. In ludic love, there is no mutual claim and no long-time commitment agreed upon by the partners. Instead it is experienced because it is fun, and when it stops being fun, the relationship is terminated.

STORGE: PEACEFUL AND SLOW

Like ludus, storge lacks passion and intensity. But whereas the ludic lover is aware of passion but keeps it under control, the *storgic lover* is unaware of any intensity of feeling. The storgic lover does not set out to find a lover but to establish a storge relationship with someone whom he or she knows and with whom he or she shares interests and activities.

Storge relationships lack passion and intensity; perhaps this is one of the reasons why they are often more long lasting.

Storgic love develops over a period of time rather than in one mad burst of passion. Sex in storgic relationships comes late, and when it comes it assumes no great importance. One advantage of this is that storgic lovers are not plagued by sexual difficulties, as are so many other types of lovers.

Storgic lovers rarely say "I love you" or even remember what many would consider romantic milestones such as the first date, the first week-end alone, the first verbalization of feelings of love, and so on. Storgic love is a gradual process of unfolding thoughts and feelings; the changes seem to come so slowly and so gradually that it is often difficult to define exactly where the relationship is at any point in time. Storgic love is sometimes difficult to separate from friendship; it is often characterized by the same qualities that characterize friendship: mutual caring, compassion, respect, and concern for the other person.

Not only is storgic love slow in developing and slow-burning, it is also slow in dissolving. Storgic lovers can endure long periods of time away from each other without feeling that there is any problem with the relationship. Similarly, they may endure long periods of relative inactivity or lack of excitement without feeling there is any relationship problem.

Mania: elation and depression

The quality of mania that separates it from all others is its extremes of highs and lows, of ups and downs. The *manic lover* loves intensely and at the same time intensely worries about and fears the loss of the love. This intense fear prevents the manic lover in many cases from deriving as much pleasure as might be derived from the relationship. At the slightest provocation, for example, the manic lover experiences extreme jealousy. Manic love is obsessive; the manic lover has to possess the beloved completely – in all ways, at all times. In return, the manic lover wishes to be possessed, to be loved intensely.

Manic lovers are often unhappy with life and so devote a great deal of energy to love. The manic lover's poor self-image seems capable of being improved only by being loved; self-worth seems to come only from being loved rather than from any sense of inner satisfaction. The manic lover needs to give and to receive constant attention and constant affection. When this is not given, such reactions as depression, jealousy, and self-doubt are often experienced and can lead to the extreme lows characteristic of the manic lover.

Pragma: practical and traditional

The *pragma lover* is the practical lover who seeks a relationship that will work. Pragma lovers seek compatibility and a relationship in which their important needs and desires will be satisfied. Computer matching services seem based largely on pragmatic love. The computer matches persons on the basis of similar interests, attitudes, personality characteristics, religion, politics, hobbies, and a host of likes and dislikes. The

Of the five types of love – ludus, storge, pragma, mania, or eros – which do you think has the best chance of lasting longest?

assumption is that persons who are similar will be more apt to establish relationships than will persons who are different.

In its extreme, pragma may be seen in the person who writes down the qualities wanted in a mate and actively goes about seeking someone to match these stated qualities. As might be expected, the pragma lover is concerned with the social qualifications of a potential mate even more than personal qualities; family and background are extremely important to the pragma lover, who relies not so much on feelings as on logic. The pragma lover views love as a useful relationship, one that makes the rest of life easier. So the pragma lover asks such questions of a potential mate as "Will this person earn a good living?", "Can this person cook?", and "Will this person help me advance in my career?" Not surprisingly, pragma lovers' relationships rarely deteriorate. This is true in part because pragma lovers have chosen their mates carefully and have emphasized similarities. Perhaps they have intuitively discovered what experimental research has confirmed, namely, that relationships between similar people are much less likely to break up than are relationships among those who are very different. Another reason for the less frequent breakups seems to be that their romantic expectations are realistic. They seem willing to settle for less and, consequently, are seldom disappointed.

EROS: BEAUTY AND SEXUALITY

The *erotic lover* focuses on beauty and physical attractiveness, sometimes to the exclusion of qualities we might consider more important and more enduring. Furthermore, the erotic lover has an idealized image of beauty that is unattainable in reality. Consequently, the erotic lover often feels unfulfilled. Erotic lovers are particularly sensitive to physical imperfections in their beloveds – a nose that is too long, a complexion that is blemished, a figure that is a bit too full, and so on. And this is one reason why the erotic lover wants to experience the entire person as quickly in the relationship as possible.

Eros is an ego-centered love, a love that is given to someone because that person will return the love. It is in this sense a utilitarian, rational love because it is a calculated love with an anticipated return. Eros is essentially hedonistic: it is a sensual love of the physical qualities of an individual; physical attraction is paramount. Eros is a discriminating type of love; it is selective in its love objects. It is directed at someone because he or she is valuable and can be expected to return equally valuable love.

AFTER YOU READ

Task 1 Reading for detail

The names given to the five different types of love in this text are technical terms and are not common words in English. Some of them might not be known to native speakers and may not appear in the dictionary. You will be able to understand what they mean only by a careful reading of the text.

Match the sentence opener on the left with its completion on the right to find a description of each type of lover.

_____ *1* The ludic lover . . .	*a*	is emotionally intense.
_____ *2* The storgic lover . . .	*b*	seeks a physically beautiful lover and an intensely physical relationship.
_____ *3* The manic lover . . .	*c*	does not seek a commitment in a relationship, just sex and fun.
_____ *4* The pragma lover . . .	*d*	is emotionally cool and seeks friendship rather than intense passion.
_____ *5* The erotic lover . . .	*e*	is most satisfied with a partner with similar needs and interests, someone who makes everyday life more comfortable.

Task 2 Test-taking: Making lists to study from

When studying a text about a group of related categories, it is a good idea to learn the terms used for these categories and make a list of the main characteristics of each one.

1➤ Look at these notes, showing in list form the main characteristics of ludic love.

> *Ludic love*
>
> *1. love is a game – not too serious*
> *2. passion kept under control*
> *3. sexual fidelity – not impt.*
> *4. no commitment – can change when no longer fun*

2➤ Make notes for *one* of the other types of love and then compare your notes with a student who took notes on the same type of love as you.

3➤ Now pair up with a student who took notes on one of the other types of love. Using your notes only, give an oral summary of the type of love that you took notes on.

4➤ Look at the different short-answer question types described on page 8 in Chapter 1. With your partner, make up three questions, one for each of the different question types, about the types of love that you took notes on.

Task 3 Personalizing the topic

1➤ Read the following questionnaire and find out what kind of lover you are. For statements that are definitely true for you, check *Yes*. For statements that are not true for you, check *No*. Check *Unsure* for statements that you are not sure about.

What kind of lover are you?	Yes	No	Unsure
The ludic lover			
If I see that a relationship is about to break up, I like to be the one to drop the other person first.	❑	❑	❑
I like to keep my lover unsure about how deeply I really feel toward him or her.	❑	❑	❑
I feel uncomfortable if someone falls too deeply in love with me and starts to get very dependent on me.	❑	❑	❑
The erotic lover			
When two people fall in love, it's like two magnets that are attracted toward each other.	❑	❑	❑
I love to see, touch, and hear the one I love as much of the time as possible.	❑	❑	❑
It's important to me that other people find my lover to be very beautiful/handsome.	❑	❑	❑
The manic lover			
If I think even for a second that my lover might be with someone else, I start to feel sick to my stomach.	❑	❑	❑
Love is so powerful that it cannot be resisted, even if the other person is married to someone else.	❑	❑	❑
When my lover and I quarrel, I get so upset that I feel sick and cannot sleep.	❑	❑	❑
The pragma lover			
If I can't have the person I want, I'll just find someone else.	❑	❑	❑
Falling or being in love is not an important thing in my life.	❑	❑	❑
One of the factors that might influence me in choosing a love is whether he or she might help my career.	❑	❑	❑
The storgic lover			
A love is true only if it lasts for a long, long time.	❑	❑	❑
I don't feel any strong need to touch or kiss the one I love.	❑	❑	❑
Two people over time may grow from being just friends to being lovers.	❑	❑	❑

2➤ Give yourself a score in each category of lover. Give yourself 3 points for each *Yes*, 1 point for each *Unsure*, and subtract 1 point for each *No*. The category of lover in which you scored the most points is the type of lover you are. A score of 9 points in any one category would be unusual and would show that you are an extreme example of that type!

PREPARING TO READ

Predicting the content

In this text you will read about the results of a survey of more than one thousand American male and female college students ages 18 to 24. The students were asked about the romantic experiences that they had had so far in their lives.

1➤ Work with a partner and predict the results for men and for women. Write your predictions in the chart.

	Average for men	*Average for women*
1 How many times have you been infatuated?		
2 How old were you when you were first infatuated?		
3 How many times have you fallen in love?		
4 How old were you when you first fell in love?		

2➤ Compare predictions with another pair of students.

3➤ In this new group of four students, tell each other how you would have answered these same questions if *you* had been asked for this information.

Speed reading

Use this text as an opportunity to practice your speed-reading skills. Before you start, review the guidelines for faster reading on page 36 in Chapter 2.

NOW READ

Now read the text "Gender Differences in Loving." Time yourself (or your teacher will time you). When you finish, make a note of how long it took you to read the whole text. Then turn to the tasks that begin on page 211.

4 GENDER DIFFERENCES IN LOVING

In our culture, the differences between men and women in love are considered great. In poetry, in novels, and in the mass media, women and men are depicted as acting very differently when falling in love, being in love, and ending a love relationship. Women are portrayed as emotional, men as logical. Women are supposed to love intensely, while men are supposed to love with detachment. Military leader Giorgio Basta noted, "Man loves little and often, woman much and rarely." Though the folklore on sex differences is extensive, the research is meager.

DEGREE OF LOVE

In their responses to a questionnaire designed to investigate love, social psychologist Zick Rubin (1973) found that men and women were quite similar; men and women seem to experience love to a similar degree. Women do, however, indicate greater love for their same-sex friends than do men. This may reflect a real difference between the sexes, or it may be a function of the greater social restrictions under which men operate. Men are not supposed to admit their love for another man lest they be thought homosexual or somehow different from their fellows. Women are permitted greater freedom to communicate their love for other women.

ROMANTIC EXPERIENCES AND ATTITUDES

In an attempt to investigate the number of romantic experiences and the ages at which these occur, sociologist William Kephart surveyed over 1,000 college students from 18 to 24 years of age. The women indicated that they had been infatuated more times than the men. The median times infatuated for the women was 5.6 and for the men, 4.5. For love relationships, there is greater similarity. The median number of times in love for these same women was 1.3 and for the men, 1.1. As expected, women had their first romantic experiences earlier than men. The median age of first infatuation for women was 13 and for men was 13.6; median age for first time in love for women was 17.1 and for men was 17.6. In this same study, men, contrary to popular myth, were found to place more emphasis on romance than women. For example, the college students were asked the following question: "If a boy (girl) had all the other qualities you desired, would you marry this person if you were not in love with him (her)?" Approximately two-thirds of the men responded no, which seems to indicate that a high percentage were concerned with love and romance. However, less than one-third of the women responded no. Further, when sociologist D. H. Knox surveyed men and women concerning their views on love – whether it is basically realistic or basically romantic, it was found that married women had a more realistic (less romantic) conception of love than did married men.

How old were you when you first fell in love?

Research seems to indicate that women more often cause the breakup of a relationship, although myth might have us believe the opposite.

ROMANTIC BREAKUPS

Popular myth would have us believe that when love affairs break up, the breakups are the result of the man's developing some outside affair. But the research does not seem to support this. When surveyed on the reasons for breaking up, only 15 percent of the men indicated that it was because of their interest in another partner, but 32 percent of the women noted this as a reason for the breakup. And these findings are consistent with the perceptions of the partners regarding the causes of the breakups as well; 30 percent of the men but only 15 percent of the women noted that their partner's interest in another person was the reason for the breakup. The most popular reason reported was a mutual loss of interest; 47 percent of the men and 38 percent of the women noted this as a reason for breaking up.

In their reactions to broken romantic affairs, there are both similarities and differences between women and men. For example, both women and men tended to remember only the pleasant things and to revisit places with past remembrances about equally. On the other hand, men engaged in more dreaming about the lost partner and in more daydreaming generally as a reaction to the breakup.

AFTER YOU READ

Time it took you to read the text _____ (to the nearest tenth of a minute, for example, 3.4 minutes).

Task 1 Reading for detail

Test your understanding of this text by reading each statement in the table and placing a check (√) in the appropriate column(s) depending on whether the statement is true for men or women or both.

	Men	Women
1 They are said to love more intensely.		
2 They show more love for same-sex friends.		
3 They have more infatuations.		
4 For a student between the ages of 18-24, the average number of times in love is less than 2.		
5 The median age of first infatuation is between the ages of 13 and 14.		
6 The median age of first falling in love is between the ages of 17 and 18.		
7 More than 50 percent say they would not marry someone if they were not in love with him/her.		
8 They more often cause the breakup of a relationship by becoming interested in another partner.		
9 They tend to remember only pleasant things after a breakup.		
10 After a breakup they tend to daydream more about the lost partner.		

Follow-up: How well did you read?

1➤ Reread the text and check your responses to the statements in the table.

2➤ Fill in the box below to calculate your reading speed in words per minute (wpm), and your percent correct in the table. A good goal would be to read at about 250 wpm with an accuracy of 70 percent.

```
a  time to read  _____
b  number of words_____667_____
c  wpm (b/a )  _____
d  number correct  _____
e  percent correct (d x 10) _____
```

Task 2 Thinking critically about the text

Discuss the following questions with a partner.

1 What surprised you about the results of the survey?
2 Do you think that researchers would get different results if they surveyed men and women in your country?
3 What were some of the questions that were probably asked in the various surveys that are reported in this text? (Write down at least four questions.)
4 How would you have answered these questions?

Task 3 Writing a summary

Read through the text again and then write a one-paragraph summary. Remember to include only the most important information.

CHAPTER 10 Writing assignment

Choose one of the following topics as your chapter writing assignment.

1 Which do you think more often accounts for why people become attracted to each other: the matching hypothesis or the complementarity principle?
2 Use the concepts in this chapter to analyze a love relationship in your life (either past or present). Discuss why you were attracted, what kind of love it was, and whether there were gender differences in the way you and your partner loved.
3 Are men and women very different when it comes to love? Try to refer to concepts from every section of this chapter (e.g., the matching hypothesis or storgic love) to answer the question.

ACADEMIC ENCOUNTERS

CONTENT
FOCUS

Human Behavior

Credits

The author and publisher would like to thank the following for permission to reproduce copyrighted material:

TEXT

Pages 5-6, 11, 15-16, 19-21, 25-27, 31-33, 37-39, and 43: from *Psychology: Being Human*, Fourth Edition, by Zick Rubin and Elton B. McNeil. Copyright © 1985 by Zick Rubin and Elton B. McNeil. Reprinted by permission of HarperCollins Publishers, Inc.

Pages 49-50, 53-54, 57-60, 65-66, 71-72, 75-77, 81-82, 85-87: from *Fundamentals of Psychology* by Josh R. Gerow, Thomas Brothen and Jerry D. Newell. Copyright © 1989 by Joshua R. Gerow, Jerry Newell and Thomas Brothen. Reprinted by permission of HarperCollins Publishers, Inc.

Pages 95-96, 99-100, 103-104, 107-108, 113-114, 117-118, 123-124, 127-128: from *Psychology: An Introduction*, Second Edition, by Josh R. Gerow. Copyright © 1989, 1986 Scott, Foresman and Company. Reprinted by permission of HarperCollins Publishers, Inc.

Page 132 (diagram): adapted from pages 472-473 of *The Interpersonal Communication Book*, Fifth Edition, by Joseph A. DeVito.

Pages 135-137, 141-143, 147-148, 153-154, 159-160, 163-165, 169-171, 175, 181-182, 185-186, 189-190, 193-194, 197-198, 201, 203-205, 209-210: from *The Interpersonal Communication Book*, Fifth Edition, by Joseph A. DeVito. Copyright © by Joseph A. DeVito. Reprinted by permission of HarperCollins Publishers, Inc.

ILLUSTRATIONS

Page 53, Figure 3.1: from "Standards from Birth to Maturity for Height, Weight, Height Velocity, and Weight Velocity: British Children, 1965 in *Archives of Diseases in Childhood*, 41, October 1966, by J.M. Tanner et. al. Reprinted by permission of the BMJ Publishing Group.

Page 66, Figure 3.2: adapted from "Youth Suicide: Predispositions,

Page 27: © Ed Wheeler/The Stock Market.

Page 31: © Laura Zito.

Page 32: © Innervisions.

Page 37: © Mark Harmel/FPG International.

Page 39: © Jeffrey Myers/FPG International.

Page 43: Gemma Comas © 1996.

Pages 45, 47: © Lori Adamski Peck/Tony Stone Images.

Page 49: © Gregg Segal.

Pages 50, 54: ©David Young-Wolff/Tony Stone Images.

Pages 57, 58: © Penny Tweedie/Tony Stone Images.

Page 59: © David W. Hamilton/The Image Bank.

Page 65: © New Jersey Newsphotos.

Page 71: © Gregg Segal.

Page 72: © David Hanover/Tony Stone Images.

Page 75: © Telegraph Colour Library/FPG International.

Page 76: © Bruce Ayres/Tony Stone Images.

Page 77: © Jim Whitmer.

Page 81: © John Terence Turner/FPG International.

Page 82: © David Young-Wolff/Tony Stone Images.

Page 85: © Arthur Tilley/FPG International.

Page 86: © Rob Gage/FPG International.

Page 87: © FPG International.

Pages 91, 93: © Julie Marcotte/Tony Stone Images.

Page 95: © Bob Daemmrich/Sygma.

Page 96: © Tom and DeeAnn McCarthy /The Stock Market.

Page 99: © Stock Montage Inc..

Page 104: © M. Siluk/The Image Works.

Page 106: *(clockwise from top left)* © Jose Luis Banus/FPG International, © Burton McNeely/The Image Bank, © Suzanne Murphy/FPG International, © Comstock, Inc., © Gregg Segal.

Page 108: © Jon Feingersh/The Stock Market.

Page 113: © UPI/Corbis-Bettmann.

Page 114: © Chronicle Features 1995.

Page 118: *(all photos)* Bernard Seal.

Page 123: © Peter Correz/Tony Stone Images.

Page 128: © Michael Krasowitz/FPG International.

Pages 131, 133: © L.O.L. Inc./FPG International.

Task Index

Page numbers in boldface indicate tasks that are headed by commentary boxes.

219